Salisbury Cathedral

The Making of a Medieval Masterpiece

Text by TIM TATTON-BROWN

Photographs by JOHN CROOK

SCALA

Salisbury
Cathedral

CONTENTS

PREVIOUS PAGE: Detail from the central high east window of 1781, depicting Moses and the Brazen Serpent (see page 120).

LEFT: The nave looking east, with the new font that was installed at its centre in 2008.

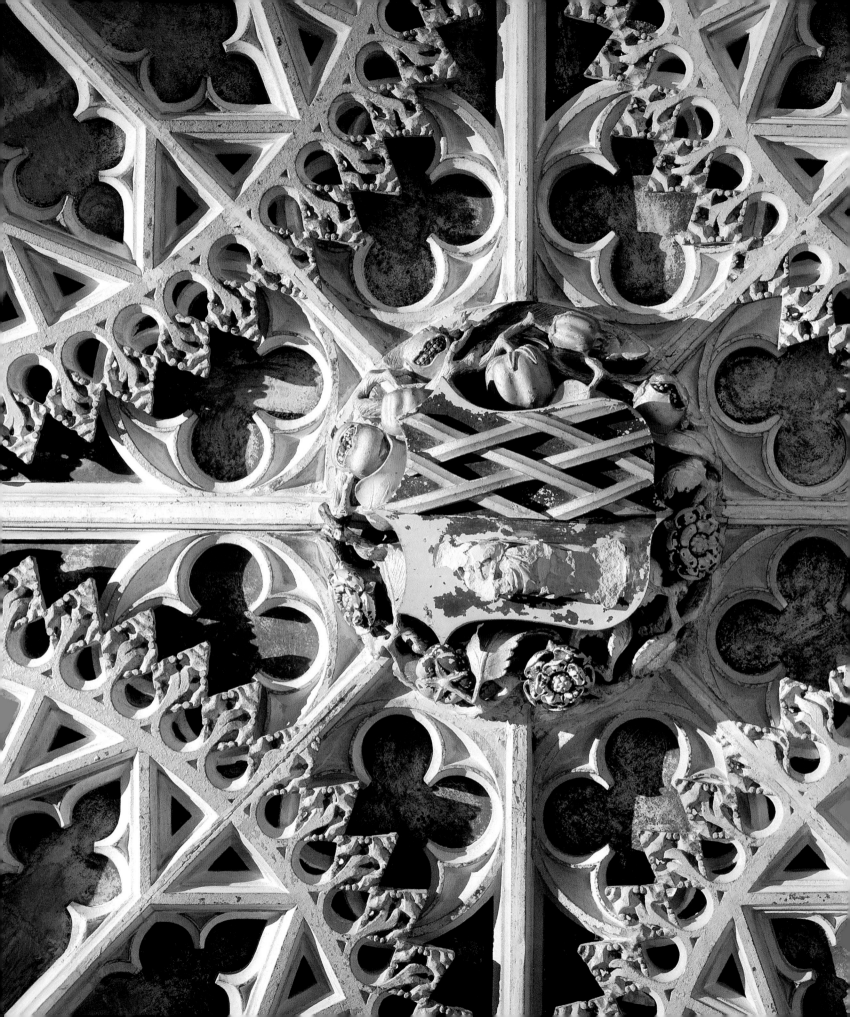

FOREWORD BY THE BISHOP OF SALISBURY

Salisbury Cathedral is a medieval masterpiece of a building recognised throughout the world. It continues to invite wonder and the worship of God, which was always its main purpose. Every time I enter the cathedral I look for something I haven't previously noticed. This popular book does a wonderful job at helping us look closely and see and understand more.

In his Foreword to the first edition, my predecessor, Bishop David Stancliffe, wrote about the ordered pattern of study, prayer and worship which were from the beginning at the heart of this cathedral's life and set in the context of a frequently chaotic medieval world. In the building's soaring pillars and arches it is as if heaven is welded to earth. Horizontally, the building's footprint is a cross, the imprint of the life, death and resurrection of Jesus:

'These were the spaces that the worship inhabited and in which the elaborate chant developed. On Sundays and Holy Days the principal Mass was preceded by a procession that visited every altar to salute the saint in whose honour it was dedicated, and toured the graveyard to include the departed members of the community, before entering under the façade of the west front, sculpted to make clear you were entering the heavenly city to join its worship.'

By the later Middle Ages the pattern of worship here – the Sarum Rite – became a template for worship in most of England. Worship has been adapted in every generation into that which is offered in the present day. The priest and poet George Herbert (1593–1633), who for the last three years of his life was Rector of Bemerton, a short walk west across the meadows, thought – like his medieval predecessors – that coming here to Evensong was to glimpse heaven on earth. Just as the building points to heaven, so does what happens within it.

Within the building there are things from every generation, from 1220 to the present day. That is a remarkable gift from something that seems so solid and fixed but has in fact changed significantly. It is fitting that this book ends with the dedication of a font in 2008. It is an invitation to each of us to become 'living stones', people living in response to the love of God. Through research and by taking care to tell the stories of the cathedral's past, the present and future also become more visible. This cathedral with a history has a lively present and great future.

† Nicholas Sarum

Early Tudor colour on the vault of Bishop Audley's chantry chapel.

1

BEGINNINGS

At the time of St Augustine's arrival in England in AD 597, the river valleys of Salisbury Plain around the empty fortified hilltop of *Sorviodunum* (in recent times, called 'Old Sarum') were still occupied by pagan Anglo-Saxons. By about 650 Christianity had arrived, and by the end of the century a large new diocese had been created, which centred on the West Saxon capital of Winchester. There, in about 648, building work began on the first cathedral in Wessex. During this time the newly Christianised Saxons were pushing westwards into British areas such as Dorset and Somerset (as they were later known), where they encountered 'Celtic' Christians who, among other things, calculated the date of Easter differently. The West Saxons continued to move further westwards and, in *c*.705, a new diocese was created for south-west England, which centred on the settlement of Sherborne. The boundary between the dioceses of Winchester and Sherborne was now defined as the forest of Selwood, which lay along the later border between Somerset and Wiltshire.

To create the new cathedral at Sherborne, Ine, the West Saxon king, brought in Aldhelm, a member of his own family who, at that time, was abbot of Malmesbury.

LEFT: North-east transept, dating to the 1230s, showing original paintings on the vaults that have been covered in limewash since 1789–90.

RIGHT: Modern statue of St Aldhelm by Jason Battle, which was installed on the west front in 2001.

He had completed his monastic education at Canterbury under Hadrian, the great Roman-born abbot of St Augustine's in that city, and had since become an efficient administrator and a very literate scholar. Bede, who must have known him, tells us of his broad learning 'in both biblical and general literature', and specifically tells us that 'he was directed by a synod of his own people to write a notable treatise against the errors of the Britons in observing Easter at the wrong time'. Aldhelm was bishop of Sherborne for only four years, as he died in 709, but a later source tells us that he constructed a wonderful church there, which was greatly enlarged over the next three centuries. In 998, it became a new monastic cathedral (run by Benedictine monks), just like the major cathedrals at Worcester, Winchester and Canterbury.

By the time Sherborne became a monastic cathedral in 998, England was under the rule of the unfortunate king Æthelred 'the Unready' (979–1016), whose country was being overrun by Scandinavian raiding parties. It is reported in the Anglo-Saxon Chronicle that, in 1003, the Danish king, Swein Forkbeard, led his men inland to sack and burn down the borough of Wilton, before proceeding to 'Sarisbury' and then finally returning down the Avon valley to his ships. ('Sarisbury' must be a reference to the hilltop stronghold at 'Old Sarum', as it is now called, which was refortified at this time. It became a small borough itself, with a mint.) Shortly after this, England was finally conquered by the Danes, with Swein (very briefly in 1013–14) taking over as king, swiftly followed by Cnut (1016–35). Danish rule came to an end in 1042, and there was once again an English king, Edward 'the Confessor' (1042–66), the son of Æthelred. He had a Lotharingian chaplain called Hereman, whom he

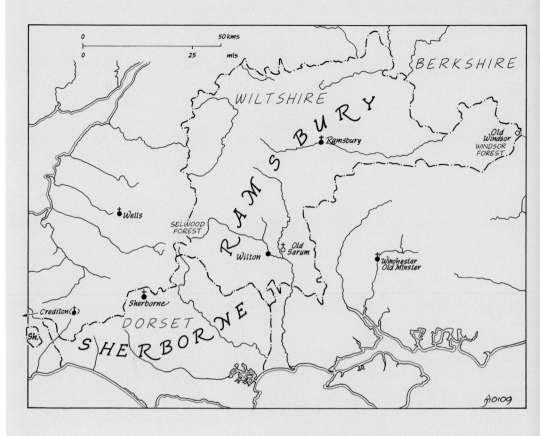

appointed bishop of the, by now, poor see of Ramsbury in 1045. Hereman tried to become abbot of Malmesbury as well, but when this failed he left England in 1055. However, three years later, after the death of the bishop of Sherborne, Hereman returned to England and was able to combine both sees, while being based in the abbey at Sherborne. His diocese now covered Dorset, Wiltshire and Berkshire, and at its extreme eastern end was Edward the Confessor's new royal residence beside the river Thames at Old Windsor.

In 1070, soon after the Norman Conquest, William the Conqueror brought the elderly Italian Benedictine monk, Lanfranc, from Normandy to be the new archbishop of Canterbury. Initially Lanfranc did not want to accept this post, but was persuaded to come to England by the new king and by Lanfranc's former pupil, Pope Alexander II. Once there, he

Map of the diocese

In 909 the vast diocese of Sherborne (covering Dorset, Somerset, Devon and Cornwall) was divided up, with new cathedrals being created at Crediton (in Devon) and Wells (in Somerset) in the same year. The diocese of Winchester, covering Surrey, Hampshire, Berkshire and Wiltshire, was divided in half, with a new diocese of Ramsbury being created on the north-west. In the 10th century, the kingdom of Wessex was also divided into shires or counties, so that Ramsbury diocese covered the new counties of Berkshire and Wiltshire, while Sherborne diocese was now quite small, covering only Dorset.

started a massive programme of reform and church building. At a council held in London in 1075, it was ordered that the bishop's seat be moved from the 'village' and monastery of Sherborne to a new church in the hilltop borough of Old Sarum. Bishop Hereman, who was now also quite elderly, had been dissuaded by Archbishop Lanfranc from resigning his see in 1071, and as soon as the move to Old Sarum had been made in 1075, he started to build a new cathedral there. The foundations of this cathedral were excavated in 1912–13, and it was found that Hereman's new building was quite small, with an overall length of only about 190 feet (58 m). The plan was a much smaller version of that used by Archbishop Lanfranc for his own new cathedral in Canterbury. This cathedral, which was rapidly built in 1071–7, was also fairly modest in scale, but it was still about a hundred feet (30 m) longer than Hereman's structure.

Unfortunately, Bishop Hereman died on 20 February 1078, when only about two years' work had taken place. It then fell to his successor to complete the building work. Osmund, a royal chaplain from Normandy, had become the king's chancellor in 1070. On becoming bishop in 1078, he gave up the chancellorship, but

View from the north-west of the excavated remains of the castle and cathedral at Old Sarum, showing the rounded apsidal east end of the cathedral, begun in 1075.

remained a key member of the king's entourage and was deeply involved in the making of the Domesday Book. On 1 August 1086, the results of this survey were presented to William the Conqueror at his new castle in Old Sarum. Not long after this, William returned to Normandy and died there a year later. Meanwhile, Osmund and his clerks continued the building work on his new cathedral and, by 1089, he had created a group of 36 canons that would serve the church of 'Sarisbury'. These men were much involved with the copying of manuscripts, and Salisbury Cathedral still has a fine collection of these, the largest group of late eleventh- and early twelfth-century manuscripts to survive in England.

The new cathedral was finished on 2 February 1091, and a year later it was consecrated by Osmund himself on 5 April 1092. Unfortunately, five days after this, due to its exposed hilltop position, it was struck by lightning and was partially destroyed. It was no doubt quickly repaired, and by the time of Bishop Osmund's death on 4 December 1099, the liturgy in the cathedral would have been flourishing. Osmund was probably buried in the centre of the canons' choir towards the east end of the cathedral nave, which was by now one of the smallest cathedrals in England. Just 25 miles (40 km) to the east, the vast new Winchester Cathedral (534 feet / 163 m long) was nearing completion as the largest cathedral in England. Its huge scale was probably an attempt to match the size of Constantine's great basilica of St Peter in Rome. It was in Winchester Cathedral that King William II (Rufus) was buried just nine months after Osmund, having been apparently killed by a keeper in the nearby New Forest.

The new king, Henry I, had a Norman priest in his entourage called Roger le Poer, who may have been his steward. In 1101,

a year after his succession, he made Roger his chancellor, and the following year he nominated him as the new bishop of 'Sarisbury'. The cathedral canons duly elected him their bishop, and in September 1102 Roger was 'invested' by Henry I at Westminster and gave up the chancellorship. Unfortunately, at this time there was a large dispute going on (over the right to appoint bishops) between the Crown and Archbishop Anselm, and it was not until 1 August 1107 that Bishop Roger was finally consecrated by the archbishop at Canterbury, after the dispute was formally resolved. By this time, he had become the king's most trusted minister and was the most important royal justice. Within a decade, he was Henry's senior minister and, while the king was away in Normandy, he also acted as regent or 'viceroy', particularly after 1120.

A 10th-century decorated Gallican psalter in the cathedral library.

Plans of the castle (left) and the cathedral at Old Sarum (right), as excavated in 1909–13. Bishop Roger's great courtyard palace is in the northern part of the castle, while Bishop Jocelin's new residence was to the north of the cathedral cloister. The aisled great hall is on the right.

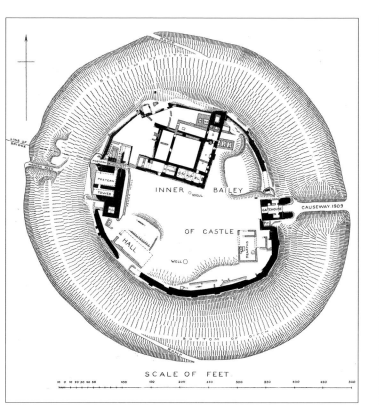

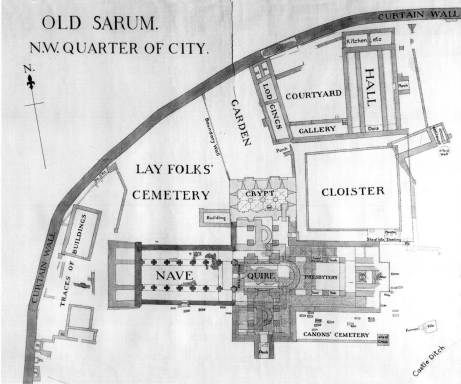

This remarkable and very powerful man obviously needed a cathedral and residences to match his status, and these he proceeded to create. At Sherborne Castle, half a mile east of the abbey, he constructed a magnificent courtyard house in the centre of the strongly fortified site. Bishop Roger was still the titular abbot of Sherborne, but this he gave up in 1122, making the prior Thurstan its first abbot. From this time until the Dissolution, the abbot would always be a canon of Salisbury Cathedral as well. Bishop Roger also built splendid new residences in his castles at Malmesbury and Devizes; a contemporary chronicler said of the latter that 'there was none finer or more splendid in Europe'.

His most important works, though, were within the castle and fortified borough at Old Sarum. In the castle he built another exceptional residence around a central court for himself and the king, while at the cathedral he demolished the small eastern arm and erected a vast double-aisled transept (like that at Winchester Cathedral) with a new choir at its centre, and to the east of this a large new presbytery and three small eastern chapels. He may have started to rebuild the nave and to erect two western towers as well. Although this cathedral was demolished in the thirteenth century, its plan was completely uncovered in 1912–13, and the bedding for many of its fine decorated floors was revealed, along with the foundations and wall-bases. The magnificence of the walls can be guessed at from the fine Romanesque architectural fragments found in 1912–13.

The new cathedral was just over 300 feet (91 m) long, with a large porch and monumental doorway acting as the main entrance to the building, which led into the south transept. On the north side of the north transept, the excavators found steps leading down into a vaulted undercroft that was contemporary with the new cathedral. This undercroft, which is still a fine feature on the site today, had three large circular pillars running down the centre to support a vault, as well as a well in the floor. It was a very secure structure, with only tiny windows in its outer walls, and it probably acted as the treasury, muniment (or record) store and vestry. Above it, and perhaps entered through a large door in the centre of the north transept, was probably the chapter house, the main meeting place of the canons, presided over by the bishop or dean.

ABOVE: Detail of a Romanesque lion's head from Old Sarum.

LEFT: Excavated Romanesque gable top from Old Sarum.

Inscribed grave-cover of Godwin, which records his ordination as a priest by Archbishop Anselm of Canterbury.

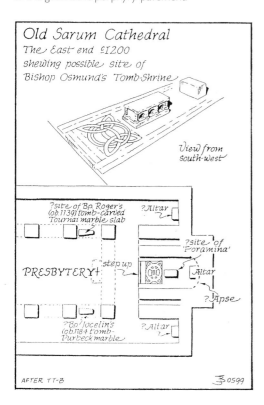

Reconstructed plan of the east end, showing the possible position of Osmund's foramina shrine east of the geometric porphyry pavement.

Old Sarum Cathedral
The East end c1200 shewing possible site of Bishop Osmund's Tomb-Shrine

View from south-west

?site of Bp. Roger's (ob.1139) tomb-carved Tournai marble slab

?Altar

?site of 'Foramina'

PRESBYTERY

step up

Altar

?Apse

?Bp. Jocelin's (ob.1184 tomb-Purbeck marble)

?Altar

AFTER TT-B

In the early twelfth century, for the first time we hear of the principal dignitaries at the cathedral: the dean, precentor (or chanter), the master of the schools (later known as the chancellor of the cathedral) and the treasurer. Quite a few of these learned men must have come from the ranks of Bishop Osmund's distinguished clerks. Many fine manuscripts were still being made here, and the precentor, Godwin, was clearly teaching a new generation of clerks to sing the plainsong that was heard daily in the choir. Amazingly, Godwin's beautifully inscribed stone grave-cover was uncovered in 1912 in the canons' cemetery against the south-east side of the cathedral, and has been kept *in situ* at Old Sarum.

East of the choir was the presbytery with an aisle on either side. The square bases for piers (which must have supported round arches) were found on either side and, set on a bench within the arches, were the traces of stone tombs. These must have held the remains of bishops Osmund (removed from the nave), Roger and later Jocelin (see below). Their elegant carved tomb-covers can still be seen in Salisbury Cathedral, as they were moved there with their coffined bodies in 1226 (see p.54).

After Henry I's death in 1135, Bishop Roger helped to ensure a smooth succession for King Stephen. However, he became caught up in the civil war with Matilda, and in 1139 all his great power rapidly disappeared. He was forced to hand over all his wealth and great castle-residences, and returned to Old Sarum a broken man, where he died on 11 December 1139. This was a sad end for an extraordinary man and probably left a cathedral in the midst of construction. We are told by a contemporary source that King Stephen stole part of the treasure left by the bishop for the roofing of the cathedral.

The next bishop, Jocelin de Bohun, was another remarkable man who was bishop for over 42 years (from 1142). He came from a powerful family, and consequently his election was initially not popular with the dean, Azo, and some of the other canons at Old Sarum. Although not a scholar, Jocelin did have much useful legal knowledge; a great administrator, he lived through most of the reign of Henry II and was involved in many of the turbulent events relating to Archbishop Thomas Becket. He failed to retrieve the bishop's castles at Sherborne, Malmesbury and Devizes, but did recover the two large manors on either side of Devizes at Cannings and Potterne. At Old Sarum he had to build a new residence (his predecessor having lost the residence in the castle there), and this he proceeded to do, immediately north-east of the cathedral, where a new cloister was created to give him covered access to a door into the north transept. Jocelin's new residence was also excavated in 1913–14, and the plan of a remarkable group of buildings was revealed. On the east was a large, 100-foot-long (30 m) aisled great hall of six bays with its main entrance and porch on the east (see plan on p.11). The dais for the bishop's seat and table was at the south end, and a passage (or gallery) led west from here to his private lodging range. Beyond this, there seems to have been a large garden.

During Jocelin's long reign as bishop, not only was the cathedral completed but also the establishment attached to it (the dean and chapter) was to reach its full later medieval form, with each canon (by now, at least 42 of them) having his own personal income from a prebend. Uniquely at 'Sarisbury', the bishop was also a canon with his own prebend, and under him was a full set of dignitaries: the dean, precentor, chancellor, treasurer, the four archdeacons, sub-dean and succentor. Each had his own endowment, with even the lowly succentor (the second singer, the precentor's deputy) having a farm at the nearby Stratford-sub-Castle given to his office. There was also a 'common fund' to be used only by the resident canons, and a detailed document (known as the *Institutio Osmundi*) was drawn up, which set out the duties and privileges of all the dignitaries.

Towards the end of Jocelin's time as bishop, we have the first documentary evidence for an incipient cult developing around the tomb of Bishop Osmund. Some early miracles were documented, and the chapel at the extreme eastern end of the cathedral was rebuilt with a remarkable geometric pavement in it (see p.13), containing purple and green porphyry (igneous rock with large inclusions). This was discovered in the 1913 excavation, and it seems likely that this chapel had at its centre the tomb-shrine of the 'Blessed Osmund', as he was now occasionally called. Remarkably, the 'foramina' tomb-

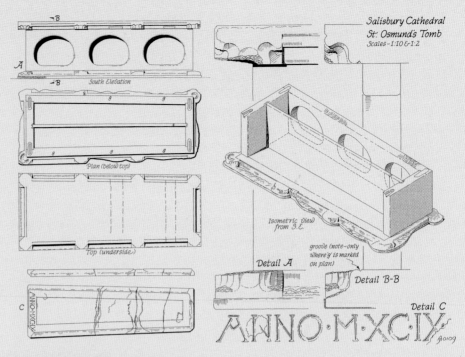

Foramina tomb-shrines

The structure above, with its large round holes in each side (for pilgrims to put their hands or heads in), was very similar in form to the tomb-shrine for St Thomas Becket, which had been made soon after his canonisation in 1173. This is shown in the stained glass just above the tomb of Hubert Walter in Canterbury Cathedral (below). Ultimately both these tomb-shrines were based on the 'Tomb of Christ' in the Church of the Holy Sepulchre in Jerusalem.

Cathedral and chapter house from the south-east, with the rebuilt 17th- and 18th-century wings of the Bishop's Palace on the right.

shrine cover, made of Purbeck marble, has survived, as it was brought down to the new cathedral with Osmund's remains in 1226. Bishop Jocelin died on 18 November 1184, having spent the last few months of his life in 'retirement' as a monk at the important Cistercian abbey of Forde, on the Dorset–Devon border. Baldwin, a former abbot of this house, had just become archbishop of Canterbury, but for the next five years the see of Salisbury remained unfilled. Finally, after the death of Henry II and the coronation of his eldest son, Richard I, in 1189, another exceptional man, Hubert Walter (then a royal justiciar and dean of York), was consecrated bishop of Salisbury on 22 October 1189 by Archbishop Baldwin. This was an extraordinary time, as Jerusalem had recently fallen to the Muslims, and King Richard and Archbishop Baldwin were

desperate to recover the Holy Land on a new crusade. After only a few months in England, Bishop Hubert also left for France and the Holy Land in early March 1190. Once there, he was a key figure in the Third Crusade, and in September 1192 he had a famous meeting in Jerusalem with Saladin, the Kurdish king of Egypt and Syria, who had conquered the Christians in 1187. After Hubert's return to England in 1193, he became archbishop of Canterbury (Baldwin had died outside the walls of Acre in 1190), one of only two bishops of Salisbury to be promoted to the archbishopric; the other was Henry Dean in 1501. A few months afterwards, another royal justiciar, Herbert Poore, was elected by the Salisbury chapter as bishop, and on 12 June 1194 Archbishop Hubert Walter came in person to enthrone his successor in the cathedral at Old Sarum.

This was the great Romanesque cathedral's final high point, having just been completed. But it was at this point that Bishop Herbert Poore and his younger brother, Richard, made the radical suggestion that a new cathedral should be made down in the valley and away from the disagreeable royal castle. The latter had dominated the small cathedral Close and restricted access to it, so had left no comfortable distance between the military garrison and the scholar canons.

Evolution of Salisbury's name

ROMAN: *Sorviodunum* ('dun' is a celtic word for hillfort)

ANGLO-SAXON: *Sarisbury* (Burh is an Anglo-Saxon word for fortified town)

MEDIEVAL: *Salisbury* (the 'r' is corrupted to an 'l' in the later Middle Ages)

2

PREPARING FOR
A NEW CATHEDRAL

As we have seen, all of the early bishops were quite exceptional men: virtually all of them were key figures in the Norman and Angevin governments in England. At the very end of the twelfth century, Hubert Walter, perhaps the most notable of them, was proving himself to be the greatest administrator of his age, as archbishop of Canterbury and justiciar of England. He inaugurated the first proper system of record-keeping at Westminster, and in 1197–8 he started to build a large new collegiate church of canons on the other side of the river at Lambeth. It was set in a 'Close' that would also contain the new London residences for both the archbishop of Canterbury and his suffragan (assistant bishop), the bishop of Rochester.

Although ultimately unsuccessful in transferring the cathedral from Canterbury to Lambeth, Walter's work was noticed by Bishop Herbert, and it is exactly at this time that Herbert started to lay out his own Close in New Salisbury. This work must have been encouraged by the archbishop, but it was actually Herbert's brother, Richard, newly appointed dean of

Salisbury, who from 1197 took the most active part. Both Richard and Herbert Poore were the illegitimate sons of Richard of Ilchester (bishop of Winchester, 1174–88), and in early 1190 Richard was a pupil of Stephen Langton – later to be archbishop of Canterbury (1207–28) – in the Paris Schools. Not long after his brother became bishop, he returned to England and became archdeacon of Dorset and a Salisbury canon, and then dean of Salisbury in 1197. In the next couple of years, the momentous decision was taken to start laying out the new Close, and probably the new town as well, down in the valley. Bishop Herbert may have initially thought of Wilton as the best place for his new Cathedral Close, but there was already a town there and a large royal nunnery (where the bishop was buried on his death in 1217). What was really needed was a much larger and completely unencumbered open site for a Cathedral Close and a new city.

The site chosen was a large gravel terrace immediately to the east of where the river Avon joined the river Nadder. This fine site

Aerial view of the Close from the south-west, with the medieval city beyond the Close walls. Elias of Dereham's house, Leadenhall (now a school), is in the bottom left-hand corner.

two and a half miles (4 km) south of the old cathedral and three miles (5 km) east of Wilton, was already part of the bishop's manorial land between the Avon on the west and the river Bourne. Two miles to the east was the much-used large royal palace of Clarendon, in its own extensive deer park, itself set within the royal forests of Chute, Clarendon and Melchet. To the south of the Avon was the large royal manor of Britford on the north-east edge of Cranborne Chase, and one can be fairly certain that King Richard I ('Cœur de Lion') was also in favour of finding a new site here for Salisbury's cathedral, and gave his consent in about 1198.

The late twelfth to early thirteenth century was a time when the population of England was increasing rapidly. It was also a time when the weather was still warm (the 'Little Ice Age' only began in the early fourteenth century), and no doubt when the Avon valley was not subjected to heavy winter flooding (though occasional flooding of the cathedral occurred from the fourteenth century

onwards!). At this time, many of the river valleys of the Salisbury plain area were filling up with settlements that spread out along the valley edges, using the natural river gravels for their common arable fields and the alluvial flood-plains for meadows. Most of the chalk downland above this area was unenclosed and would soon be populated with large numbers of sheep.

As well as this, some completely new towns were being created; the closest to Salisbury (only five miles / 8 km to the south) was the one laid out a few years before 1208, for Bishop Peter des Roches of Winchester, in his large manor of Downton. This remarkable plantation was a very broad marketplace, half a mile (just under 1 km) long, extending from the Salisbury Road on the west to the bridge over the Avon at Old Downton. At Stockbridge, William Brewer created a similar half-mile-long marketplace over meadowland, which was situated halfway between Salisbury and Winchester; it was granted a market by Richard I. These were ambitious schemes, but the new town planned for Salisbury was on a much bigger scale and would be laid out on a grid, or chequerboard, plan (each square in Salisbury was called a 'chequer'). However, the starting point for the new town was the large new Close (of about 80 acres / 32 hectares) placed in the south-west corner of the new town, on the edge of the gravel terrace. At its centre was a roughly rectangular walled enclosure, some 800 feet (240 m) long by 600 feet (180 m) wide within which the cathedral was to be built. This enclosure was to become the 'sacred space' at the heart of the new foundation, and it was soon consecrated and eventually contained a large number of burials. Around its perimeter a road was built, beyond which large messuages (house-plots) for the bishop, dean and about

Plan of the Salisbury area in the 13th century.

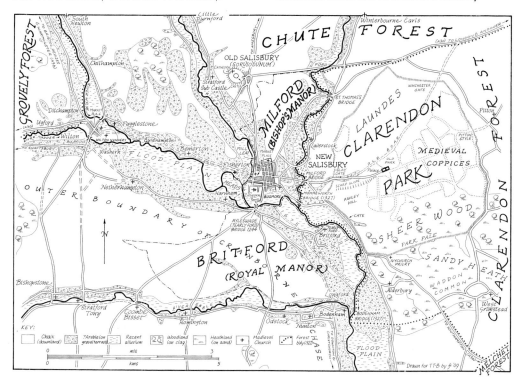

twenty canons were marked out. We first hear of these just before 1200, when a canon called Peter of Blois, the archdeacon of Bath, wrote apologising for not being able to attend the distribution of messuages. He said, 'let us go down joyfully to the plains, where the valley abounds in corn, where the fields are beautiful, and where there is freedom from oppression'. This last comment referred to the many difficulties caused particularly by the royal garrison in the castle at the centre of Old Sarum.

Unfortunately, after the death of King Richard and the succession of his younger brother, John, in 1199, the move down the hill seems to have stalled, although it is likely that the creation of the large new town continued apace. Bishop Herbert was on good terms with King John, but after the latter's excommunication by the Pope in November 1209 the bishop went into exile in Scotland. By the time he returned to England in 1213, he was an infirm old man and was not involved with Magna Carta at Runnymede in 1215, or in the chaotic events at the end of John's reign. His younger brother, Richard, was by then bishop of Chichester (1215–17), and was perhaps rebuilding the semicircular east end of the cathedral there, as a larger, new rectangular structure with three new chapels. This is exactly what he did at Salisbury a few years later, on a much grander scale.

During the early part of John's reign, Dean Richard Poore was working very hard to prepare the chapter for its move. His endeavours can be seen, in particular, in his work with the liturgical practices and customs of the cathedral, which came to be called 'Sarum Use'; this would have a very strong influence on the liturgy at all the other secular cathedrals in Britain. Dean Richard also wrote a new *Ordinale* (order of services), which described in detail all of the liturgical arrangements for

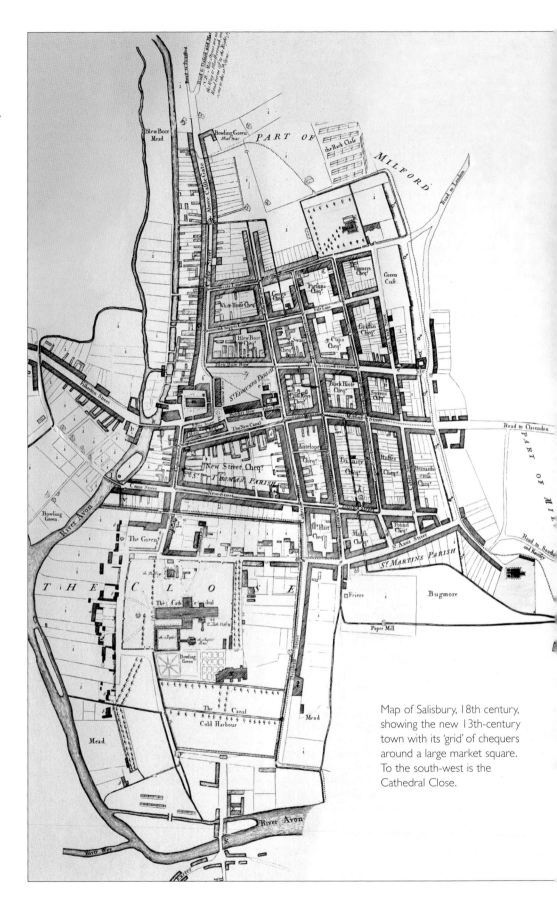

Map of Salisbury, 18th century, showing the new 13th-century town with its 'grid' of chequers around a large market square. To the south-west is the Cathedral Close.

the cathedral, and it is very clear that in the early thirteenth century all of this was being practised in the cathedral at Old Sarum. In fact, by using the Customary, it is possible to work out exactly how all the different services and processions took place in the old cathedral. One can even suggest the dedications of each of the different altars in the building. Dean Richard must have been very sad, therefore, when Pope Innocent III put the whole of England under an interdict on Sunday 23 March 1208. This involved a complete suspension of all ecclesiastical rites. So, for the next six years, virtually all services in the cathedral at Old Sarum would have ceased. Meanwhile, Richard returned to Paris where, as a highly respected teacher and *magister* at the schools (university), he would lecture on the Bible. In this he was following his old master, Stephen Langton, whose appointment as archbishop of Canterbury (and a cardinal) by the Pope, and its rejection by King John, had caused the papal interdict.

King John finally submitted to Pope Innocent III in May 1213, and Archbishop Stephen Langton returned to England in July, followed by Richard. Both Richard and his elderly brother, Herbert, therefore returned to Salisbury to restore the chapter and its services in the cathedral, when the interdict was finally lifted in 1214. Richard was enthroned bishop of Chichester in early January 1215, the year of Magna Carta, and he attended the Fourth Lateran Council in Rome, which started on 1 November 1215. In 1216, he was one of the executors of King John's will, and early in 1217 he helped secure John's nine-year-old son's position on the throne. By now Bishop Richard was at the heart of both ecclesiastical and secular politics in England.

On 7 January 1217 Bishop Herbert died, and his brother was suggested as his successor by the whole chapter, formally becoming bishop of Salisbury in June 1217. There was still a period of crisis in England, but, despite this, almost immediately after Bishop Richard's arrival in Salisbury, moves were made to start the building work for the new cathedral.

Bishop Richard now showed why he was not only a great scholar and royal servant but also one of Salisbury's greatest bishops and the true founder of its wonderful new cathedral. Supported by the chapter, he sent a letter off to the new pope, Honorius III, in March 1217, which sought formal approval for the move to the new site. Famously, the letter also gave a list of reasons as to why the old cathedral was so badly sited: it was dominated and oppressed by the castellan (the castle governor) and soldiers of the royal castle; they were not allowed to go in or out without permission from the castellan; the faithful were not permitted to visit the church (the nave of the old cathedral was by now a much-used parish church for Old Sarum); there were not enough houses for all the canons; the many strong winds made such a noise that they could hardly hear their own chanting; in winter they suffered from colds and rheumatism; there were no trees or grass there, and consequently they were blinded by the glare of the white chalk; and, finally, water had to be brought up from the river at Stratford-sub-Castle, at great expense. Guala, the papal legate in England, was instructed to investigate and quickly sent a report to Rome supporting the move, and on 29 March 1218, formal approval was granted by the pope.

As we have seen, the new Close had already been laid out and it seems likely that some of the canons were already building their houses there. Bishop Richard also started to build himself a large new residence in the Close, called 'New Place',

and fragments of this building still survive within the Bishop's Palace (now the cathedral school). He then called for a chapter meeting of all the canons on 2 July 1218. The move was unanimously agreed and fund-raising for the new building was then discussed. Many gifts of materials (particularly from the Crown) would no doubt be forthcoming, but huge sums of money would also be needed. This would be for the labour force particularly, and it was clear that large numbers of people were now coming to the new city to live and trade, and to be part of, and provide services for, the workforce for the new cathedral.

The canons comprised an exceptional group of men, and Bishop Richard soon persuaded them to give up a large part of their annual prebendal income for an initial seven years. At this July 1218 meeting, no doubt the bishop would have told the canons about the great council of Westminster he had attended in May, which finally resolved all conflicts and brought peace to England, and how he had gone to Worcester Cathedral for a great ceremony of consecration on 7 June 1218, and had been given a relic of St Wulfstan. There was also a new bishop at Worcester, William of Blois, and it was the consecra-

tion of the new shrine for St Wulfstan – the great Norman bishop who had been canonised by Pope Innocent III in 1203 – that was taking place. Close by the shrine was the brand new tomb of King John. St Wulfstan had been a close colleague of Osmund, and Bishop Richard almost certainly now started to plan a new shrine for 'Saint' Osmund (he was not yet canonised) at the east end of the new cathedral. Worcester returned the compliment by starting to build a fine new eastern arm in 1224, based on the new eastern arm just begun at Salisbury.

The chapter meeting on 2 July, which agreed the contributions for seven years from all the canons (including those who were absent!), had pledged that a first quarterly payment 'without quibbling or fiddling' should be paid on All Saints Day (1 November). Now, at last, the work could commence in the spring of 1219. As we shall see, it was probably at this time that the plan of the new cathedral was marked out on the ground and the digging of the foundation trenches was started. A new temporary wooden chapel had to be built rapidly; the building work for this began on 8 April and the finished chapel was consecrated on Trinity Sunday (2 June 1219). This chapel would have been in the new churchyard, which was also dedicated on Trinity Sunday.

In February 2003 part of a wall foundation and fragments of the basal course of

LEFT: Choir and presbytery of Worcester Cathedral, which follows closely Salisbury's early Gothic style. King John's tomb is in the centre.

Upper part of the carved Purbeck marble effigy of King John (c.1230) on his tomb in Worcester Cathedral. His head is flanked by miniature effigies of St Oswald and St Wulfstan. The marble may have been carved in Salisbury.

Statue of Elias of Dereham made in 1946 and now displayed south-west of the crossing. Elias's large pair of dividers in his right hand are very 20th century.

stones were found just beneath the paving at the north side of the crossing in the cathedral (see plan on p.30). This could have been part of the north wall of the temporary chapel, which must have been made large enough to accommodate choir stalls as well as the temporary altar of the Virgin Mary, where the bishop celebrated his first mass on Trinity Sunday. In this position, under the later crossing, it would have been completely inside the outer walls of the new cathedral being laid out at this time, and quite far to the west of the three eastern chapels that were to be completed first.

The rest of 1219 was probably spent laying the foundations for the whole cathedral, as well as preparing for all the masonry work to begin in the spring of 1220. Large masons' lodges and places for the carpenters and smiths would have been constructed. There would have also been places within the churchyard where flint, rubble and stone were being stockpiled, and the building of several of the canons' houses and the bishop's 'New Place' was also being carried out. It was also suggested to the chapter that a formal 'transmigration' from old to new Salisbury would take place on 1 November 1219; it is recorded that this was unanimously agreed by Bishop Richard, Dean Adam, Precentor William, Chancellor Hugh and Treasurer Abraham, as well as the canons present. All these events, dating from 1217 to 1229, are vividly chronicled for us by the precentor William de Waude in his *Historia translationis veteris ecclesiae beatae Mariae Sarum ad novam*. William became dean in September 1220, just after the death of his predecessor. Dean Adam was probably one of the last people to be buried at the old cathedral. We also learn from William de Waude's account that Bishop Richard now realised that the amount of money subscribed so far was not nearly sufficient, and it was agreed that seven canons should at once set out to raise funds in different parts of the country, even though it was now winter. Precentor William was sent to London, while the chancellor, Master Hugh de Gaherst, went to Winchester. Others went further afield – one even went to Scotland.

After a chaotic decade, England was now settled and at peace. Many new building projects were contemplated, although the project for a new Salisbury Cathedral was by far the most ambitious. During the winter of 1219–20 two other important projects were also getting underway: at Westminster Abbey work had begun on a new large Lady chapel, while at Canterbury a magnificent new shrine for St Thomas Becket was being made. The designer of the latter was a very remarkable man called Master Elias of Dereham, who was Archbishop Stephen Langton's steward and a canon of Wells and Lincoln. The historian Matthew Paris called him one of the two 'incomparable artificers' of the shrine of St Thomas. Matthew Paris also tells us that, during this time, Bishop Richard 'laid out spacious foundations on the advice of famous new artificers, whom he had invited from distant parts, and he had himself laid the first stone'. Elias was newly returned from exile in France, and it was almost certainly at this time that Bishop Richard persuaded him to come to Salisbury as a canon. A Salisbury *Martyrologe Booke* (seen by the early Tudor historian John Leland, but now lost) tells us specifically that Elias of Dereham was 'rector of the new fabric of the church of Salisbury from its foundation for 25 years'. He died in 1245 and this perfectly matches with the first major phase of building work. With the engagement of Elias of Dereham, perhaps early in 1220, all was now ready for the main work to start.

3

THE FIRST PHASE

One of the myths about Salisbury Cathedral is that it was built on a marsh or swamp: in fact it was built on a well-drained gravel terrace, just above the alluvium of the river valley. In winter the groundwater level rises, but only very occasionally does it flood. The top of the hard, well-sorted gravel terrace, which is currently about four feet (1.2 m) below ground level, is also at about the level of the summer water table, and it is to this level that the foundations were dug. The gravel terrace, which makes an excellent uniform natural raft foundation, is about 28 feet (8.4 m) thick and lies on top of the natural upper chalk. Salisbury, unlike nearby Winchester Cathedral, is therefore exceptionally lucky in having almost perfect conditions for the building of a huge new masonry structure, and amazingly the added spire, which is

LEFT: The three eastern chapels viewed from the north-east, which were completed by 1225. The large flying buttresses above, filled with perpendicular tracery, date from 1398.

Subsidence at Winchester Cathedral
Salisbury was spared the subsidence problems that bedevilled Winchester Cathedral, visible here in this photograph from 1905 – the south wall (right) is leaning out dangerously and the vaulted ceiling is cracked. Potential catastrophe was averted at Winchester in 1906–11 using a diver working in water-filled trenches underneath the foundations to shore them up with concrete.

over 400 feet high (over 120 m), sits on a foundation that is only four feet deep. The stone spire was not, of course, part of the original plan, but one can be fairly certain that a large masonry building about a hundred feet (30 m) high, with stone vaults throughout, was planned from the start, so a very good foundation was essential.

Once the papal licence had reached England from Rome in the early summer of 1218, it is likely that Bishop Richard would have had the plan of the whole new cathedral laid out on the ground, within the walled enclosure that was to become the churchyard. The boundaries of this enclosure, which may have been marked out in 1198, are only roughly aligned north, east, south and west. By contrast, the new cathedral was very accurately set out to the points of the compass, and we can be sure that special care was taken to find true north using the sun. At Old Sarum, a large cloister was added to the north-east side of the cathedral in the mid-twelfth century, and on this new site it is almost certain that a cloister was planned and set out at the start. At Old Sarum the fairly irregular cloister had overall dimensions of *c*.120 by *c*.140 feet (36 by 42 m), while the new cloister here was laid out on a more generous scale, with overall dimensions of 170 feet (51 m) square. This was probably the first thing

ABOVE: Statue of Bishop Richard Poore, 1946, south-east of the crossing. Anachronistically, he is holding a model of the whole cathedral, with tower and spire!

OPPOSITE: View of the cathedral from the north-east, showing the 13th- and 14th-century spirelets and pinnacles, as well as the tower and spire.

RIGHT: Late 19th-century statues of the Virgin and Child, with censing angels, in the porch above the west doorways. The smaller heads above are original.

LEFT: View east from the presbytery to the aisled Trinity Chapel behind the high altar.

ABOVE: Aerial view from the north-west, showing the cathedral within its large graveyard. The Bishop's Palace is top left.

to be marked out on the ground, as it was to abut the southern churchyard boundary near the bishop's house. At Old Sarum too, the bishop's residence had been adjacent to the cloister.

Once this was done, the main east–west axis for the cathedral itself could be accurately laid out some 250 feet (75 m) north of the southern boundary wall. This did not place the new cathedral at the centre of the enclosure, no doubt because much space was needed on the north for the lay cemetery, with a large freestanding bell-tower at its centre. From the very beginning, Bishop Richard's plan for his new cathedral was on a massive scale. The two great monastic cathedrals at Canterbury and Winchester were exceptionally long by now, with each being some 550 feet (165 m) in length.

But only at Canterbury had a very large new eastern arm and liturgical space been created, with secondary eastern transepts (for more altars) and an exceptionally large choir, presbytery and eastern Trinity Chapel for the shrine of St Thomas Becket. At Lincoln, Bishop Hugh of Avalon had started to create a fine new liturgical space at the east end of his cathedral, and this project was now continuing, particularly after Bishop Hugh's own canonisation in 1220. Lincoln and Canterbury perhaps had the strongest influence on Salisbury's new plan, although Lincoln still had a polygonal east end at this point (like Canterbury), and what Bishop Richard wanted for his new east end was a large rectangular central chapel, which would be flanked by two lesser chapels. This sort of structure had recently been created at

Winchester, although the unstable ground conditions never allowed its completion there. Also, by this time, Bishop Richard had probably started to build this form of east end at his much smaller cathedral at Chichester.

Now, at last, Bishop Richard had a unique opportunity to create a completely new cathedral on a virgin site. In laying out the plan of the building, he probably started with the least important, but most regular part – the nave – with its position already determined by the cloister to the south. This block plan, which was some 475 feet (142.5 m) long overall, must have been worked out some time before, but only now, in 1218, was it being marked out on the ground.

Original foundation trenches

The nave is exactly 200 feet (60 m) long from the centre of the west wall to the start of the crossing, and these limits on the west and east were probably the first two north–south baselines to be marked out. Next, the four principal crossing piers' positions were established, followed by the eastern chapel spaces in the greater transept. After this, the central space for the choir (planned to contain over a hundred stalls) was marked out, followed by the eastern crossing and transept. Then the 55-foot-long (16.5 m) presbytery was delineated for the liturgical space around the high altar. Finally, the space for the lower (in height) eastern chapels was marked out with a north–south ambulatory at their west end.

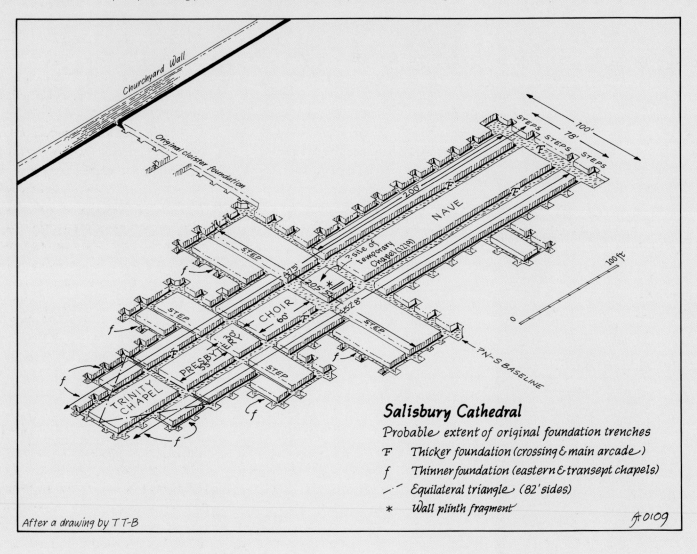

Salisbury Cathedral
Probable extent of original foundation trenches
F   Thicker foundation (crossing & main arcade)
f   Thinner foundation (eastern & transept chapels)
- · -   Equilateral triangle (82' sides)
*   Wall plinth fragment

After a drawing by T T-B

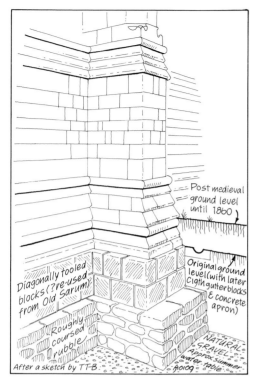

ABOVE: Sketch showing a portion of the two foundation levels that were made for the cathedral.

BELOW: Detail of a buttress plinth on the north side of the cathedral. The top of the foundation is also exposed, since the top of the 1860 concrete apron is a few inches below the 13th-century ground level.

Immediately after this was done, the principal foundation trenches were carefully positioned and digging got underway. The foundation trenches for the outer walls of the main building, with their continuous system of external buttresses, were the largest. These were about six to seven feet (1.8–2 m) wide, as were those of all the main internal arcades. The trenches of the eastern chapels (and perhaps those of the transept chapels) were only about five feet (1.5 m) wide. As we have seen, the foundation trenches were then all dug down about four feet (1.2 m) until the top of the hard gravel surface was reached. This was a huge job and one can assume that a large labour force was gathered to start work during 1218. As the straight-sided trenches were dug down to the natural gravel, they were filled straight away with two feet (60 cm) of rammed rubble set in yellow lime mortar. Piles of the rubble for this, mostly made up of flints, would have been made already in the churchyard, and the lime-mortar was being mixed nearby. To make the lime, large quantities of chalk were burnt in kilns, using timber for the fires. There are several early references to the king that suggest he donated many trees for the purposes of making lime, from Panshet Wood in the south-east of Melchet Forest (just to the north of the New Forest). The chalk for making the lime may have come from the closest source on the north side of Harnham Hill, just to the south-west of the cathedral.

As soon as the lowest foundation had been made, the upper section of the foundation was constructed using up to two courses of masonry for the outer faces. This masonry is fairly rough, and its top can now be glimpsed in many places around the outside of the cathedral. This is particularly noticeable on the north of the nave, where it was re-exposed in the later

nineteenth century; this is when the level of the churchyard was greatly reduced (and a concrete apron was built, with a gutter, all around the building). The blocks for the upper part of the foundation were often made of Hudcott stone, and the quarries at Hudcott (in the upper Greensand), some eight miles (13 km) due west of the cathedral, are still the nearest local source of building stone for the site. This stone was much used in the twelfth century for masonry buildings in the south Wiltshire area (at Old Sarum, for example), but as we shall see, it was not considered good enough (nor hard enough) for the masonry of the new building. The axe-cut diagonal tooling on the blocks of the upper foundation also suggests that these blocks were reused from twelfth-century buildings, including, most likely, the buildings at Old Sarum, which were already being demolished by 1218.

Once the four feet of foundations had been made, no doubt with a very accurately levelled top surface, the exact positions of the outer and inner faces of the walls could be very carefully marked out on the foundation top using string-lines, set-squares and a large pair of compasses – tools that are shown in contemporary thirteenth-century manuscripts. This was a critical stage, because only now could the first courses of beautifully cut masonry be very carefully laid, and once they were in place, it would fix the plan of the building for all the future work.

If one examines the lowest courses of masonry all around the outside of the cathedral, a very distinct moulded plinth will be seen with a pronounced batter (slope). At the top of the plinth is a large roll-moulding, and near the bottom, on only the second course of masonry, another roll can also be seen. Inside the nave of the cathedral is a bench that runs all the way around the walls, which has its own

THE FIRST PHASE

roll-moulding immediately beneath it, and the top of this bench is at the same level as the top of the lower roll outside.

These lowest two courses, outside and inside, were not only the first courses of the new masonry to be built but also they were laid in such a way that suggests the masons started at the west end of the nave and then moved eastwards. This is most clearly seen in the greater transept, where the bench has to step up into the area in which the new eastern chapels were to be situated. A second step was made within the eastern transepts so that in the chapels at the east end, the bench (and, of course, the floor level) was about a foot higher than in the nave. (See plan on p.55.)

In terms of its floor levels, Salisbury Cathedral is about the flattest cathedral in England, but from the very beginning steps were made as one moved eastwards, first into the choir (and greater transept chapels) and secondly into the presbytery (and eastern transept chapels). Later, more steps were created in the eastern part of the presbytery to raise the high altar up to a much higher level, although all of this was destroyed in 1789–90 during James Wyatt's restoration, and was only partly replaced by during the great nineteenth-century restoration of Sir George Gilbert Scott.

What the first builders were doing was laying out the lowest courses of masonry for the whole building so that a fill could be put into the choir and presbytery straight away to create the proposed slightly raised floor levels. Only when this had been done could they start to erect the first of the higher walls at the east end, where we know, from William de Waude's account (as mentioned on p.23), the main construction started in 1220.

ABOVE: Detail of the internal bench, with the roll-moulding rising up at the step in the greater north transept.

RIGHT: Sections through the lower wall and top of foundation in the nave and eastern arm.

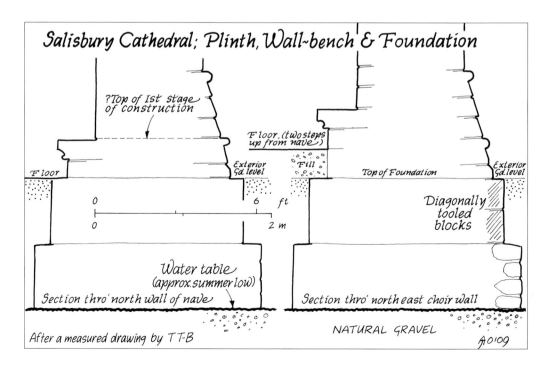

Salisbury Cathedral; Plinth, Wall-bench & Foundation

?Top of 1st stage of construction

Floor, (two steps up from nave)

Floor

Exterior Gd. level

Fill

Top of Foundation

Exterior Gd. level

Diagonally tooled blocks

0   6   ft

0   2 m

Water table (approx. summer low)

Section thro' north wall of nave

Section thro' north east choir wall

NATURAL GRAVEL

After a measured drawing by T T-B

However, it seems clear that a great deal of the work mentioned above was taking place in 1219, and the large labour force continued to work on the foundations and the lowest sections of the walls. It was at this time also that the lowest walls of the monumental north porch were being laid (which has an internal bench with a roll-moulding beneath it), and all the other proposed doorways were being created, including those into the north-west and north-east corners of the cloister. The

former was subsequently blocked up and replaced by another doorway further west, when the cloister was enlarged (see p.55). There were also original doorways into the outer western corners of all the transepts, which led into short passages connecting with the spiral staircases (or vices). These stairs were soon to become important as the main access to the higher levels of scaffolding. Careful scrutiny of the lowest walls reveals other smaller doorways that were blocked up in the later thirteenth

ABOVE: The north doorway into the nave from the north porch.

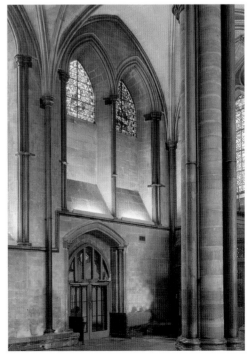

RIGHT: Later doorway from the south-west corner of the nave into the cloister, showing how the window above has been modified and partly filled in where the cloister vault abuts it. The earlier, now blocked doorway was just to the left.

century; these must have been made for the workmen only. One is towards the east end of the south choir aisle, while, leading to the outside, another very small blocked doorway can be seen at the base of the spiral stair in the south-east transept. A much larger blocked doorway on the south-west side of the greater north transept (now filled with the Harris family monument) was almost certainly created as the main entrance into the eastern arm from the north, before the nave and north porch were completed.

By the end of 1219, it seems likely that the plinth and internal wall-bench had already been built for the whole of the cathedral. Only on the west front, with its larger outer stair-turrets, are there indications that its form had not been fully worked out at the very beginning. The next stage was to acquire large numbers of rectangular blocks for the ashlar masonry of the completely plain walls above the plinth and below the next set of mouldings. This would bring the walls up to about nine feet (2.7 m) above the ground. Remarkably, there are eight courses of masonry above the plinth top, and though each course has a different height, the same coursing is continued unbroken until the second bay of the nave, which suggests that the lowest part of the outer wall of the eastern arm was being constructed in the first stage of building. It is also noticeable that, although each block has been very accurately cut to fit the coursing, quite a large number of different types of stone were used. This suggests that at the beginning of the work, stone was being acquired in large quantities from all available sources. Only a little later in the higher work, as we shall see, was a single main type of building stone from near Tisbury being used.

The need to bring the height of the plain wall to nine feet above the ground was carefully calculated because the ritual connected with the placing of consecration crosses on the walls of churches (as defined in Roman and English Pontificals) stated that there should be three consecration crosses on each of the four cardinal faces, both inside and out (in other words, 24 in all), and that they should be ten palms above the ground. A palm, from wrist to fingertip is considered to be 9 inches, making ten palms 7½ feet. At almost exactly this height, one can see three very fine consecration crosses set into the top of the plain walling at the east end of the cathedral: one in the centre and two on the faces of the outer buttresses. Three more are visible on the north side: two on the outer buttresses of the greater transept and one on the centre buttress of the eastern transept. The Salisbury Cathedral external consecration crosses are undoubtedly the finest and most elaborate set of such crosses ever made in Britain. Even more surprisingly, there appears to be a contemporary account of when they were put in place.

In William de Waude's account of the commencement of the building work at the new cathedral, he tells us that on St Vitalis the Martyr's day (28 April) in 1220, a day already decided for this, Bishop Richard came 'with great devotion, with a few earls or barons of the county, but with a very great multitude of the common people, coming from all parts'. A service was then held (presumably in the temporary chapel) 'and the grace of the Holy Spirit was invoked'. Then the bishop:

… putting off his shoes, went in procession with the clergy of the church to the place of the foundation (*fundatio*), singing the Litany; then the Litany being ended, and a sermon first made to the people, the bishop laid the first stone for the Lord Pope Honorius, who had granted licence for translating the church

Blocked up external doorway to the spiral staircase in the south-west corner of the south-east transept. It was probably made for workmen's access to the upper scaffolding.

External cross (1220).

Consecration Crosses

Close examination of the external crosses shows that they are each made from a single carved disc of stone, just over two feet (60 cm) in diameter, and that they must have been put in place at the same time as the plain ashlar. The mortar joints between all the blocks are very thin indeed, showing that they cannot have been inserted later. The outer face of the stone disc is surrounded by a roll-moulding with a quatrefoil inside it. Within this can be seen the shallow indent for a floriated brass cross, with the remains of fixing holes, some of which still contain lead dowel plugs. Sadly, all the original brasses that were fixed there have gone (perhaps removed in the 17th century), as has the original colour. The internal crosses, however, were made by cutting chases into existing ashlar masonry for the bronze crosses and painting the surrounding area with a foliated quatrefoil pattern. Behind the altar in the Trinity Chapel, the traces of original colour are still visible on the masonry (below right), uniquely with no brass. Elsewhere the crosses have been repainted in strong 20th-century colours (below left). These internal crosses were probably first made in 1258 for the consecration of the cathedral.

Internal crosses (1258).

of Salisbury; the second [stone] for the Lord Stephen Langton, archbishop of Canterbury and cardinal of the Holy Roman Church at that time with our Lord the King, in the Marches of Wales. Then he added to the new fabric a third stone for himself. William Longespée, earl of Salisbury, who was then present, laid the fourth stone, and Ela Devereux, countess of Salisbury, the wife of the said earl, a woman truly praiseworthy, because she was filled with the fear of the Lord, laid the fifth. After her certain nobles added each of them a stone. Then Adam the dean, William the chanter, Hugh the chancellor, Abraham the treasurer, and the archdeacons and canons of the church of Salisbury, who were present, did the same amidst the acclamations of the multitude of the people weeping for joy, and contributing thereto their alms with a ready mind, according to the ability which God had given them. Later, when the nobility had returned from Wales, several of them came thither, and laid a stone, binding themselves to some special contribution for the whole seven years following.

This great event had clearly been planned for some time, and Bishop Richard must have been very disappointed when he was told at a late stage that the king and much of his court could not attend, as they were involved in important negotiations with the Welsh at Shrewsbury. He had already organised a 'great store of provisions' for the large feast that he had planned for after the ceremony, but more of the common people would undoubtedly have benefited from this.

The most important thing about William de Waude's account for our understanding of the actual construction work is his reference to the 'placing of stones at the foundation'. This may have been only the

large rectangular blocks of masonry, but the specific reference to numbered individual stones does perhaps suggest something more, and the uniquely splendid stone discs with consecration crosses on them would fit the situation very well. The three most important stones laid for the Pope, the archbishop and the bishop were perhaps the three crosses in the east wall, while the earl and countess of Salisbury's stones could be the crosses put on the buttresses of the greater south transept. The stones laid by the other lesser nobles and by all the members of chapter were perhaps just ordinary blocks of ashlar masonry. On the south-east buttresses of the greater south transept is a unique consecration cross consisting of an elaborately carved cross on a lozenge-shaped block. The significance of this is not known, but it could just possibly be the stone laid by Countess Ela since, much later on, lozenges were used heraldically for women.

William's account also tells us that 1220 was an exceptionally memorable year because, just over two weeks after the

Drawing by John Constable, 1820, of the carved lozenge-shaped consecration cross on the south-east buttress. This unique stone may have been laid by Countess Ela.

OPPOSITE: The east wall of the Trinity Chapel, showing the three external consecration crosses.

laying of the stones at Salisbury on the eve of Whitsunday (Saturday 16 May), the foundation stones for the new Lady Chapel at Westminster Abbey were laid. The following day (Whitsunday itself), Henry III was properly crowned in the abbey (his earlier hurried coronation in 1216 had been in Gloucester Abbey). The third great event, on Tuesday 7 July, was the translation of the body of St Thomas Becket from the crypt of Canterbury Cathedral to the magnificent new shrine in the Trinity Chapel there. The previous evening, Bishop Richard had been given the special job of being Archbishop Stephen Langton's main assistant at the opening of the original tomb of St Thomas. The designer of the new shrine was Elias of Dereham, and with

the completion of the new shrine of St Thomas and its inauguration on 7 July 1220, he could now turn his attention fully to the construction of the new cathedral.

On his return to Salisbury after this momentous event, Bishop Richard had to deal with a potential financial crisis at home. Funds were slow in coming in, particularly those that had already been promised, but it was essential that as much money as possible was raised, so that the very expensive main building work could commence. A general chapter meeting was held on 16 August, and draconian measures were agreed for dealing with canons who were major defaulters. If promised contributions were not received within fifteen days, then agents would be sent to seize the

crops in the fields of a defaulting canon's prebend. For prebends further afield (outside the Salisbury diocese), the defaulting canon would be suspended from his right to go into the church, and he might even be excommunicated.

A week after this chapter meeting, Dean Adam died suddenly, while visiting his own manor at Sonning (on the Thames near Reading). This required another general chapter to be summoned to elect a new dean, and much acrimonious discussion then ensued. The bishop, as a canon, tactfully declined to use his own vote, and after much further debate, William de Waude was himself elected dean. These meetings were probably held in the chapter house at Old Sarum, and after his election William tells us that he was led to the church (presumably the old cathedral) and prostrated himself in prayer before the high altar, before being taken by the bishop to his stall in the choir, and then to the dean's seat in the chapter house. That day he ate with the bishop, he proudly tells us.

Despite all these distractions, it seems very likely that there was significant progress in the building work in 1220. Not only were the lowest sections of the outer walls of the whole eastern arm being built, but also the upper walls and the large lancet window-openings in the three eastern chapels were starting to be constructed. The masonry shell of the bishop's fine new residence must have been nearing completion because, on 9 May 1221, the king gave the bishop twenty 'couples' (pairs of timber rafters) from his park at Gillingham (in Dorset) to make his hall at New Salisbury. On 30 December of that same year, ten more 'couples of oak' from Melchet Wood were given to the bishop by the king 'to make his chamber'. The chamber was on top of the vaulted under-croft that still survives today, and which is immediately to the west of the great hall.

4

BISHOP RICHARD'S 'NEW BASILICA'

Once the ceremony for the laying of the stones on 28 April 1220 was over, work must have progressed rapidly on building the three eastern chapels. For this, a whole series of 'lodges' or 'shops' were put up for the stonemasons, marblers, carpenters and smiths. Later there were also workshops for the plumbers (workers in lead) and the glaziers. The principal building stone for the cathedral was always said to have been Chilmark stone. However, this is unlikely, as most of the best stone from the Chilmark ravine (twelve miles / 19 km west of Salisbury) came from underground mines, and there is no evidence for these mines being used before the post-medieval period. A mile or two south-west of Chilmark, in the Tisbury area, a very similar building stone known to geologists as the 'lower building stones', can be found at the surface, and this is the most likely source of the stone used for the medieval cathedral. To the south of the river Nadder, near Place Farm (a large grange belonging to the abbess of Shaftesbury), are the remains of ancient waste from long-abandoned quarries, and these are now most noticeable, as 'hills and holes' on Dumpling Down. Sadly no documentary evidence survives for the thirteenth-century quarrying work, but in the mid-fifteenth century, the dean and chapter recorded the giving of presents to the abbess of Shaftesbury, for the use of her quarry at Tisbury. Nearby a modern quarry at Upper Chicksgrove is extracting similar stone for most of the present-day repairs to the cathedral.

LEFT: Salisbury Cathedral from the south-east, with the Trinity Chapel in the foreground.

RIGHT: Map of the Tisbury area, showing the source of the principal stone used at Salisbury Cathedral.

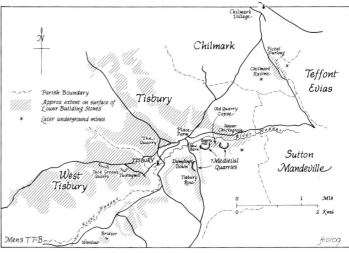

RIGHT: Detail of the slender Purbeck marble shafts that support the vaults in the Trinity Chapel.

It is very likely that a large new operation was set up in the Tisbury area in about 1219 to provide all the new stone for the cathedral. Probably several hundred banker-masons worked here almost continuously for the next 30 or 40 years. Stone quarrying has continued sporadically in the Tisbury area until the present day, helped in the nineteenth century by the arrival of the railway. From Tisbury, the river Nadder flows as a small stream all the way to Salisbury; thus it is far too small (and was always flanked by water-mills) ever to have been used as a means of transport. We must imagine, therefore, an almost continuous procession of large carts drawn by oxen, which would have carried the blocks of stone to the Cathedral Close at Salisbury, a distance of about eighteen miles.

As soon as the plain ashlar masonry of the outer wall of the cathedral reached about nine feet (2.7 m) above the ground, a new stage began with the making of the mouldings at the base of the lowest level of windows. These windows were simple in form, with paired openings between the buttresses in the north and south walls, and triple openings above the altars in the east walls. Externally a series of stone mouldings was made below the sills and on the neighbouring buttresses, but the putting in of a continuous, deeply cut moulding of Purbeck marble marking the inside of the base of the large splayed sills was a technique used in the building for the first time. Soon afterwards, a series of Purbeck marble bases were placed on the wall-bench inside, and as the main wall was built up, vertical shafts of Purbeck marble were fixed in place with Purbeck

Purbeck marble

Purbeck marble is not a 'true' marble in the geological sense, because in the 19th century a marble was defined as a metamorphosed limestone, which means that the stone has been transformed under great heat and pressure to form a much more crystalline stone. (Carrara marble in Italy is the best-known example of this.) The 'marble' for Salisbury was sourced from a place called Dunshay (or Downshay), which is in the Isle of Purbeck in Dorset. John Leland (who had seen early documents) tells us that Alice Bruer, from Dunshay, supplied all the marble for the cathedral for the first twelve years, and near the ancient manor house at Dunshay today, it is still possible to see a long strip of disturbed ground running east from it. Modern excavations further east have revealed how the marble occurs in the ground in thin beds of limestone (only about two feet (60 cm) thick) within large areas of shale. Produced in large swamps at the very beginning of the Cretaceous period, the limestone itself is a freshwater limestone full of very small snails (called *Viviparus*), which can still be seen clearly in the marble in Salisbury Cathedral today. The marble also contains layers of a type of oyster (called *Unio*), and sometimes even small fragments of dinosaur bones. The footprints of dinosaurs (particularly the *Iguanadon*) are also found in the shale on the bottom of some of the marble beds.

marble capitals at the top, held in place by more Purbeck marble.

The use of Purbeck marble to mark the horizontal and vertical lines in the cathedral was soon to become a dominant feature of the new building, so much so that there is now more Purbeck marble in Salisbury Cathedral than in any other building in Britain. This remarkable material was first used in this way in England, on a very small scale, for cloister arcades and in the Rotunda of the new Temple Church in London, in the middle of the twelfth century. But from the late 1170s it was being used in large quantities, in the rebuilt eastern arm of Canterbury Cathedral around the new early Gothic choir and presbytery. This was clearly the inspiration for Salisbury, and it is certain that Bishop Richard wanted this from the start. It is possible to suggest that the new architectural elements for the cathedral, incorporating large amounts of Purbeck marble, were now being worked out in drawings and on a tracing floor in the master mason's lodge. The details of the mouldings and geometry were probably worked out by the master mason, but the overall design was presumably made by Elias of Dereham (the 'custos' or 'rector' of the fabric), who was now living in the Cathedral Close. He is sometimes known as 'the architect' of Salisbury Cathedral, but 'architect' is really a post-Renaissance term and a better, but cumbersome, title might be 'designator' or designer.

In the Middle Ages marble was defined as just a stone that could be polished, as opposed to the definition that was to come later (see box, opposite). In the early thirteenth century there was a special group of workmen at Salisbury that used sharp sand (perhaps with sheep's fleeces) to polish the marble. Purbeck marble was also used unpolished at Salisbury Cathedral, and this can be seen in the blocks (or

drums) making up the large pillars throughout the buildings. The largest quantities are in the four great piers around the crossing, which ultimately hold up the tower and spire.

Another very large workforce was brought together at Dunshay, to extract and rough out all the blocks of marble for the cathedral. Also, at this time, many other pits were being opened up along the very narrow limestone outcrop, which ran eastwards to Swanage. This was to supply a growing industry in south-east England, and much of the marble must have been shipped out from jetties in Swanage Bay. The Purbeck marble for Salisbury, though, was most likely transported overland in ox-carts and, from 1220 for about 50 years, vast quantities of the roughed-out marble blocks would have been taken there.

As soon as the first loads of Purbeck marble reached Salisbury, one of the principal activities of the marblers was to produce the large numbers of polished shafts that were used in the building; in the new Trinity Chapel, at the east end of the building where the work started, are found the most slender shafts of all. They were used to form exquisitely slender arcade-piers to give the Trinity Chapel its own miniature aisles, and they were used on the outer walls. There can be little doubt that Bishop Richard and Elias of Dereham had planned this beautiful space from the beginning, not only to contain the first major altar in the building but also to have, at its centre, a completely new shrine for 'St' Osmund, the not yet canonised early Norman bishop (see p.55).

To put in the very narrow columns of Purbeck marble, carefully moulded bases were made at the bottom, upon which were fixed the long, thin shafts (each in two pieces), and the moulded capitals at the top. Naturally, scaffolding was needed, as were the services of the smiths, who made the small iron dowels to join the shafts together and to the capitals and the bases. Above the capitals of the freestanding piers, an iron tie-bar (still visible, see p.49, but often not noticed) was inserted, which held the shafts in place, before the centring (timber framework) for the first vaults could be put in. Working alongside the smiths, for the first time, were the plumbers who poured molten lead into the ironwork and stone joints. By this time, it was once again well known (as it had been in classical times) that if the iron rusted, it would expand and split the masonry. Close examination of the Purbeck marble, just above the joints, shows the place of a small hole made in the marble, through which the molten lead was poured.

Around the outside of the joint is a thin brass ring, which was almost certainly an original feature. As we have seen, brass was also used in the consecration crosses, so right from the beginning three different types of metal were used at Salisbury, each having its own specialist artisan, and each an expensive commodity sourced from a considerable distance. The lead may have come from the Mendip Hills of Somerset, but the source of the iron and bronze (a copper-tin alloy, called 'latten') is unknown.

All these workmen needed workshops close to the cathedral, although they may have lived on the new messuages in the city. However, a small amount of documentary evidence survives, which tells us about some of the workshop sites. Two documents of 1219–20 refer to land belonging to the *carpentaria* (probably the carpenter's shop or lodge). This land is said to have belonged to Godard the Carpenter (possibly the master carpenter) and Cecily, his wife. There is also a charter describing a messuage belonging to Master Nicholas of Ely, 'our mason', who was probably the master mason. His messuage is said to be 'outside the canons' enclosure', which situates it between the Trinity Chapel and the bishop's new residence. This charter, dated 1220–7, also gives the messuage's dimensions – 10 perches and 4 feet in length by 7 perches and 4 feet in width (which is 169 by 119½ feet / 50.7 by 35.8 m) – which fit well with the available space to the east of the cloister. This area is now mostly within the grounds of Salisbury Cathedral School.

OPPOSITE: Terry Ball's cutaway reconstruction of the three eastern chapels, as completed by 1225. The vaults and roofs would have been finished by this date, but here they are shown as a cutaway. Note the temporary partition and the doorway (later blocked) in the wall on the right.

BELOW LEFT: Purbeck marble capital in the vestry, showing lead in a 'pouring hole'. Note how the excess lead has flowed out of the shaft's top.

BELOW: Brass rings surrounding the joint between five shafts in the Trinity Chapel, behind which is an iron tie.

Salesbury Cathedral . Trinity Chapel C. 1242
Reconstruction Tim Tatton Brown - Drawn Tony Bell Sept. 2008

The results of the masons' skilled work can still be seen clearly at the cathedral, but something that is less apparent is the important work of the carpenters. We have already seen that they were on site at a very early stage, to build the temporary wooden chapel in 1219. If one looks closely at the masonry of the walls, it is possible to see also the positions of small square holes, called putlog holes (literally 'put log') where the horizontal timbers of the scaffolding were placed. This gives some idea of the scaffolding timber that was put up one 'lift' at a time by the carpenters.

By 1222 the upper walls of the three eastern chapels must have been nearing completion and, as we have already seen, the Purbeck-marble shafting of the Trinity Chapel was being put in place. The carpenters would now have the difficult task of putting in centring for the first time, on which the quadripartite ribbed vaults would be built. The geometry of all the vaults would have to be accurately worked out on the ground, and the masons and carpenters would then work together closely, so that the wooden centring would perfectly match the elaborately moulded ribs that were now being prepared. At first sight, the architectural detailing of Salisbury Cathedral looks fairly plain and simple; for example, there is very little carved foliage work. However, the mass of deeply cut mouldings used on the rib-vaults would require a great deal of preparation by the masons, and it is at the east end of the cathedral – in the Trinity Chapel and ambulatory area – that the mouldings are most elaborate. Only in this area is a form of 'nail head' decoration added to the ribs as an extra decoration.

Francis Price's perspective view of the original roofs of the three eastern chapels, before he reconstructed them in 1736.

As is well known, and for obvious practical reasons, the roofs of large medieval masonry buildings were usually put on and covered before the stone vaults were put in beneath them. However, in the Trinity Chapel (and perhaps elsewhere in the cathedral), the roofs could not be built until the vaults were in place. This is because the three original parallel roofs over the Trinity Chapel (removed in 1736) could not be put in place until small low walls had been built on top of the vaults, which are above the arcades and between the central space and the narrow side aisles. The work was obviously continuing rapidly, so there was always the risk of heavy rain showers filling up some of the vault-pockets.

Plate 12. to face Page 27.

E.Price Del. 1747 *P.Fourdrinier sc*

A Perspective View of the termination of the Isles, with S.t Mary's Chapel, at the East extremity of the Church.
Dedicated by Bishop Beson on Michaelmas Day 1223, as may be seen Page 11 and 12 of this Work

Although the present roofs above the Trinity Chapel were completely rebuilt by the cathedral surveyor (and clerk of works) Francis Price in 1736, most of the original roof timbers do still survive over the chapels of St Peter and St Stephen on either side. These roofs were drawn and carefully studied during repair work in 1998, and the opportunity was also taken to sample the oak timbers for dendrochronology (tree-ring dating). Remarkably, the skilled dendrochronologist Dr Dan Miles was able to show that some of the timbers were actually felled in the spring of 1222,

and that much of the timber originated not in England but in south-east Ireland. Later it was found that many more of the oaks used in the roofs and doors of Salisbury Cathedral between the 1220s and 1250s came from Ireland (no doubt at King Henry III's behest), which had been recently conquered by England. We also have one piece of documentary evidence for this, in the Patent Rolls for 1224, where there is a record of a cargo of timber for the cathedral works being carried on the Western (in other words, Irish) sea by William of Dublin. Other

evidence would suggest that the timber was being taken across the sea from Dublin to Bristol, before being carried overland to Salisbury. This Irish oak is of exceptional quality, as is the carpentry itself. Many of the carpenters who made the roofs were probably specially brought in for the work (so were, no doubt, the skilled carver masons), and it is interesting to note that they sometimes marked the roof trusses with Arabic, rather than Roman, numerals. This is a very early use of Arabic numbers in England, especially among artisans.

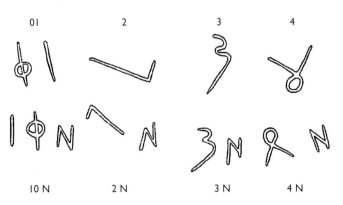

One of the early 13th-century carpenters' marks, using Arabic numerals (left). Some of the others are shown in a sequence in the drawing above, made by Dan Miles.

Wenceslaus Hollar's engraving of the east end in c.1660, showing the original form of the eastern chapel roofs. On either side are the late 15th-century chantry chapels.

The early 1220s was a very busy period in the Salisbury Close, because not only was the cathedral being built but also fine new stone houses for the canons were being erected on the messuages around the churchyard. A chapter meeting in August 1222 reviewed the position of non-resident canons, and reduced their annual period of residence from three months to 40 days. However, more pressure was put on them to start building a house, and they were told that they must get their own building work underway by Pentecost 1223, or the bishop and dean would force this upon them. In 1224 the chapter ordered that the traditional celebrations at the beginning of Advent (during which much drinking was done) should not take place in an individual canon's house but in a suitable common hall, where the fire did not smoke! This could have been an early hall for the vicars (canons' deputies) to use for their daily meals.

By the beginning of 1225, the construction work on the three eastern chapels was almost finished, and it was perhaps in the spring and summer that the sheets of lead were put on the roofs. Large timber-frames were also constructed by the carpenters, which would slot into all the lancet windows of the chapels (some 27 of them in all). These had both horizontal and vertical iron bars put into them, and once the frames were fixed into the masonry, a series of large, mainly rectangular panels of glass were fixed in place with more lead. These panels would have been put on to the window-frames from the outside. We do not know if the stained-glass artists were already working on the site in 1225, or whether simpler glass was put in at this

New lead roofing sheets on the nave triforium and porch, applied in 2000. They follow closely the form of the original lead roof coverings. Note also the timber-frames with the leaded glass set into them, in the lancet windows above.

time. However, by the early 1240s, all the windows in the cathedral would have contained elaborate stained glass, including perhaps a Tree of Jesse in the central eastern light. Inside the chapels the walls and vaults would have been painted mainly with red and green patterns (both simple red-line patterns and more elaborate foliage decoration). An impression of what this looked like can still be gained in the Trinity Chapel, as this decoration was roughly repainted in a simpler way (though with Victorian pigments) in the later nineteenth century, after G. G. Scott's restoration (see p.124). Traces of the original painted decoration can still be seen on the aisle vault to the west.

William de Waude's account resumes in 1225 under the heading 'New Basilica'. It tells us that Bishop Richard: '... saw that the fabric of the new church of Salisbury has, with God's help, got to the stage where divine service could be celebrated there in a fitting manner, and he was filled with great joy, for he had committed both money and hard work to this great construction project.'

He goes on to tell us that, on Sunday 28 September, the bishop dedicated the altars in the three eastern chapels of the cathedral, and that the arrangements for the use of these altars were formally agreed a few days later by the chapter. From this day until the Reformation, the principal eastern altar, although dedicated to the Holy Trinity and All the Saints, was used for the daily mass of the Blessed Virgin Mary; the bishop undertook to provide the endowment needed for this to be done, 'in perpetuity'. Bishop Richard also said that he would retain the altar, and all the offerings at it, under his own control for the next seven years, so that all the money could go to the fabric fund.

The next day, Michaelmas Day, the archbishop of Canterbury, Cardinal

Some of the reconstructed grisaille glass.

Stephen Langton, preached an inspiring sermon to the people and celebrated mass at the new altar. Many lay magnates and six other bishops were also present, and Bishop Richard entertained all of them for a week in the newly completed great hall of his palace next door. Three days later, on 2 October, Henry III arrived with many more magnates and they were also all lavishly entertained by the bishop. Now, at last, the first stage of the new cathedral was complete and, as we are told, it was in the architectural form of a 'basilica', meaning a double-aisled hall. At the centre of this basilica, Bishop Richard wanted to create a new shrine for 'St' Osmund. Despite his best efforts, this was not achieved in the following few years, and when he was eventually appointed reluctantly as the bishop of Durham in 1228, the canonisation had not yet taken place.

King Henry III was clearly very impressed by what he saw at Salisbury, and a few years later he encouraged the building of a similar but larger 'basilica' on the east side of the new Temple Church in London. In 1231 he decided that he wanted to be buried there. After 1245, however, he started the colossal rebuilding of Westminster Abbey, which was ultimately to be his place of burial.

OPPOSITE: The new 'Basilica': Trinity Chapel looking east, with its slender Purbeck marble columns. Two candles on the floor flank a black marble slab, marking the site of the shrine of St Osmund. The glass in the east window was only installed in 1980. Its blue colour is very different from the medieval blue.

5

THE EASTERN ARM, CHOIR AND PRESBYTERY

With the consecration of the three eastern chapels, a temporary blocking wall was put in on the west side (see p.43), and work could now continue on the building of the much larger eastern arm. By the end of 1225, it is likely that the building of the outer walls was already well in hand, and that the Purbeck marble piers in the presbytery and choir had already been erected. The large area to be enclosed here was about 145 feet (43.5 m) long and 39 feet (11.7 m) wide, and over this space, the first of the much larger high vaults and roofs were to be constructed. The height of each level above the floor was carefully worked out, and then the elevations' geometry must have been drawn out on a large tracing floor on the ground.

The height of the main arcade had already been determined when the eastern chapels were built, and the level of this and the vaults was maintained throughout the rest of the building. The top of these vaults, and the level of the long Purbeck-marble string-course above all the main arcades, is about 42 feet (12.6 m) above

LEFT: Elaborate mouldings in the north-east corner of the presbytery.

RIGHT: High east window above the Trinity Chapel roof. The masonry for this was probably erected in 1230. On either side of the high east wall are 'secret' spiral staircases, which can only be seen from the upper levels.

the ground; the next two stages (now known as the triforium and clerestory) were to double this. The top of the high vault and the central lancet windows in the clerestory were to be some 84 feet (25.2 m) above the floor, with the highest external masonry reaching to almost 90 feet (27 m) above the ground. Compared with contemporary cathedrals in France such as Amiens, where the top of the high vaults reached over a hundred feet (30 m) above the ground, this was not very high. In England, however, this must have seemed exceptional. Only at Westminster Abbey, some 30 years later, would the high vaults reach to just over a hundred feet above the ground.

Some evidence for the situation at the end of 1225, when the king was again at Salisbury, comes from an entry in the Close Rolls, dated 30 December, which records that thirteen 'long straight oaks for making cranes (*vernas*)' were given to Elias of Dereham from the king's small park at Odiham (Hampshire), 'for work on the church at Salisbury'. Does this indicate that the new cranes were being built that

winter, so that a start could be made in the spring on the new work at the upper level? It is also worth noting that when the highest wall was built with the triple east window in its upper section, its outer corners were made with stair turrets in them, presumably to give direct access to new high-level scaffolds.

On 7 March 1226 the great local magnate William Longespée, earl of Salisbury, who had only recently returned from Gascony, died in the castle at Old Sarum. The following day his body was brought down to the new Trinity Chapel, and he had the honour of being the first person to be buried at Salisbury, in the 'New Basilica of the Blessed Virgin', as Dean William (de Waude) once again calls it, in the presence of the bishops of Salisbury and Winchester, and many of his fellow earls and barons. Three months later, on Sunday 14 June (Trinity Sunday), William recorded the 'translation of the bodies of the three Norman bishops, from Sarum Castle to the New Fabric, that is the body of Blessed Osmund, the body of Bishop Roger and the body of Bishop

LEFT: Painted effigy of William Longespée, on a later 13th-century painted wooden tomb-chest. Originally over his grave in the Trinity Chapel, it has been in the nave since 1789.

ABOVE: Eastern arm which shows, looking north-east, the three levels. Behind the choir and altar run the aisles, above which comes the triforium with plate-tracery in the upper part of the arches and 14th-century flying buttresses behind. Highest of all is the clerestory.

Grave covers

Remarkably, three 12th-century stone coffin lids still survive in the cathedral, although, owing to the destructive reordering in 1789–90, they no longer cover the coffins and bones of the three bishops. The first of these covers is of black Tournai marble (a polishable carboniferous limestone from modern Belgium), and it is carved in a rich Romanesque style of the mid-12th century. For some unknown reason, later in the Middle Ages, the original head of the bishop was replaced by a new mitred head of Purbeck marble. This must be the tomb-cover for the great Bishop Roger le Poer. It is worth noting that both his nephews, Bishop Alexander of Lincoln (d.1148) and Bishop Nigel of Ely (d.1169) also had Tournai marble funerary slabs over their tombs in their respective cathedrals, so it is possible that they provided the slab for the cathedral at Old Sarum, some years after Bishop Roger's rapid fall from grace and death in 1139. The second grave-cover is a wonderful carved Purbeck marble slab of a bishop in a later twelfth-century style. Down the centre and around the edge is a long Latin inscription that declares:

> They weep today in Salisbury for the sword of justice, the father of Salisbury's Church is dead. While he was strong he cherished the unfortunate and did not fear the arrogance of the powerful but was a scourge, the terror of evil-doers. He took his descent from dukes and nobles, and like a jewel reflected glory on the three princes of his house.

Translation by Daphne Stroud

These two fine 12th-century grave covers were brought from Old Sarum in 1226. Bishop's Roger's (left) is made of Tournai marble (with a later Purbeck marble head), while Bishop Jocelin's grave cover (right) is inscribed Purbeck marble. Note the many fossil oysters visible on the surface.

F. Raby's 1947 drawing of the inscription on Bishop Jocelin's grave cover.

Jocelin'. No further details are given, but this must have been an important event too, with a great procession to accompany the heavy stone coffins and their equally heavy, decorated stone lids, from Old Sarum to the new cathedral.

In the past it has been suggested by some that this was a new effigy for Bishop Osmund, but modern scholarship can show that it must relate to the long-lived Bishop Jocelin, who was born into a noble house, unlike Osmund, and died in 1184.

The third tomb-cover, by contrast, was clearly made to cover a shrine, and this exceptional survival of a tomb-shrine must have been made in the later twelfth century to cover the first shrine of Blessed Osmund at Old Sarum. Sometimes described as a 'foramina' shrine (see p.14), there can be little doubt that it was placed carefully on the arcade bench on the south side of the new Trinity Chapel, so that it could soon be opened and the relics could be translated to a magnificent new shrine at the very centre of the chapel. Unfortunately, Bishop Richard's great efforts to achieve the canonisation of his predecessor were unsuccessful, and it was not until 1457 that Osmund was canonised and the shrine was finally built. Throughout the years 1225–7, Bishop Richard was not only driving on the building work at Salisbury, but he was also heavily involved at the royal court, where Henry III (still only nineteen years old) assumed full power in January 1227. Bishop Richard was also famous as a conciliator, and in the early 1220s he had tried to help resolve the conflicts between the bishop and monks at Durham Cathedral. After the sudden death of the bishop there in 1226, Pope Gregory IX finally translated Bishop Richard to Durham in May 1228.

Everybody in Salisbury would have regretted Bishop Richard's move to

ABOVE: The foramina shrine that originally covered the grave of Blessed Osmund. It was returned to the south side of the Trinity Chapel in 1999.

BELOW: 13th-century building phases with original doorways and altars, and the original plan of the cloister.

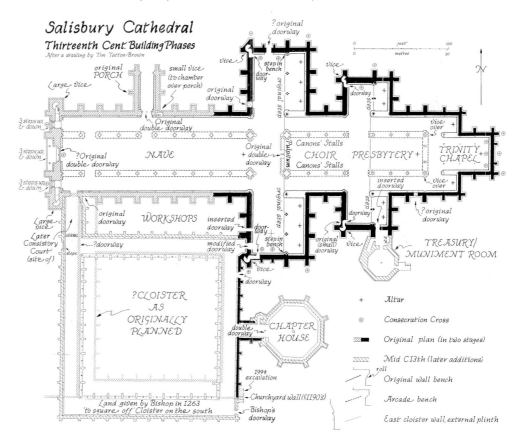

Durham hugely, but, with the king's permission, the chapter quickly put in hand the process of electing his successor. This was done in the new Trinity Chapel and Robert de Bingham was chosen, a noted theologian, who had been at Oxford and possibly Paris. He was the Salisbury canon holding the prebend of Slape, and was elected on 9 September 1228. Because Archbishop Stephen Langton had died on 9 July, the king asked for papal confirmation of his election, and this was sent before the end of the year. The full documentation of this election survives with a list of the 40 canons who 'consented and subscribed' to it. At the head of the list were Dean William; Roger of Salisbury, the precentor, who would become bishop of Bath and Wells in 1244; Robert of Hertford, the chancellor, who became dean in 1236; and Edmund of Abingdon, the treasurer, who was elected archbishop of Canterbury in 1233, and would himself be declared a saint in 1246, the year Bishop Robert de Bingham died. All were exceptional men. With this election, our most detailed historical source comes to an end, but the story can be continued with other documentary sources.

Robert de Bingham was another great bishop of Salisbury, and his eighteen-year period of office saw the completion of the entire eastern arm of the cathedral, a remarkable achievement in its own right. Matthew Paris tells us that he furnished the choir with its stalls and glass, and provided 'the lead roofing of the front of the church'. The 'front' in this case is not the west front but the eastern arm. He is also well known for paying for the

very fine, new double stone bridge over the Avon, on the south side of the Close, and for rebuilding the neighbouring St Nicholas' Hospital. Appropriately, Bishop Robert's beautifully carved Purbeck marble effigy lies in the position of honour on the north side of the high altar.

During the next few years, after Bishop Robert's consecration in 1229, local people would have noticed the inner walls becoming considerably higher; they would have seen also the exceptionally striking triforium arcades being constructed at the base of these upper walls. Once again a very large number of Purbeck marble shafts (and capitals and bases) were needed for the compound piers. It is also notable that, above these piers, openings were made that display the use of tracery for the first time. This is sometimes called 'plate-tracery' because of the way the elaborate quatrefoil- and octofoil-moulded openings are cut through the flat surface. In the east wall, above where the high altar was to be, a remarkable series of five openings was made, that, uniquely, has tracery carved from Purbeck marble rather than stone. In the upper part of the triforium, another new feature was introduced: a splendid series of carved heads, which act as the corbels supporting the Purbeck marble shafts leading up to the springing points for the high vaults. The carved heads are themselves a superb portrait gallery of many of the prominent local people. Of course, we cannot put names to them, but there are clues – since many of the heads wear mitres and some (including a female one), a crown. The Purbeck marble capitals above these corbel heads are also

Bishop Robert de Bingham's effigy

The effigy was only returned to this position north of the high altar in G. G. Scott's restoration in 1870, having been displaced during the late 18th-century restoration. There has been some muddle over the attribution of the effigy and, for a time in the 18th and 19th centuries, it was supposed to have covered Bishop Richard's tomb. However, we now know for certain that Bishop Richard was buried in 1237 at Tarrant Crawford in Dorset, where he had ended his days in the Cistercian nunnery he had founded at his birthplace. The effigy is certainly mid-13th century in style and can only have covered Robert's grave.

OPPOSITE: Some of the corbel heads in the triforium, of bishops (with mitres), a king (possibly the young Henry III) and a high-status young woman.

exceptional, as they are the first in the cathedral to all be given foliage decoration.

Behind the glorious triforium façades, the hidden inner wall faces above the aisle vaults are naturally all plain, but are nevertheless made with ashlar masonry, not simply rubble. Here it is possible to see all of the original flying buttresses that were inserted into this wall to transfer the loads from the high vaults to the tops of the buttresses on the outer walls. To the ordinary visitor, these flying buttresses are almost invisible because their sloping top-sides are immediately beneath the aisle roofs. They can, though, be seen at close hand by the modern visitor to the roof-spaces, from catwalks over the aisle vaults. Between each of the bays created by the flying buttresses, a series of three beautifully made oak roof trusses was put in to support the aisle roofs, and on the north side of the cathedral almost all the original roof trusses survive. (On the south, many were replaced in the eighteenth century.) Once again, recent dendrochronology tells us that much Irish timber from the Dublin area was used. The trusses themselves are extremely well made; the distinguished historian of medieval carpentry, Cecil Hewett, described them as 'the finest lean-to roofs surviving in any English cathedral'. Almost all the joints are close-fitting mortice-and-tenon joints, but in one place there are a few notched-lap dovetail joints, which reflect the great change in carpentry joints from lap-joints to mortice and tenon that was taking place in the early Gothic period.

Above the triforium level was built the slightly thicker clerestory wall with a continuous passage in it. This contained a sequence of triple lancet windows in each bay, in each case the central lancet being taller than those on either side. This was a sort of 'trademark' feature of the architecture probably associated with Elias

of Dereham. Away from Salisbury it can be seen most famously in the new 'basilica' at the London Temple Church, and in the archbishop's chapel at Lambeth. It can also be seen, unusually, at the east and west ends of the parish church at Potterne near Devizes. Potterne was the prebend held by Elias of Dereham from 1220 to 1245, and this beautiful miniature Salisbury Cathedral must be his gift to the place that gave him his handsome prebendal income of 50 marks a year. Potterne Church must have been built during the 1230s. In 1232 Elias also gave the house he had built for himself – in the west walk of the Close – to the bishop for succeeding canons. It was called Leadenhall and had been built as an exemplar for other canons' houses. Sadly most of it was demolished in 1915 (see p.16).

By about 1234, much of the masonry of the eastern arm was nearing completion and the high roofs were being planned. More Irish timber would have been used, but there is also an entry in the Close Rolls for 22 January 1234, which records the munificent donation by the king to the dean and chapter of 200 large trees (called *fusta*) from the forests of Gillingham, Savernake, Chippenham and Dean (some of the trees from the Forest of Dean did not arrive until 1236). These were almost certainly for the high roofs. Most of the high roofs for the eastern arm were rebuilt 500 years later in 1736, but over the north-east transept the massive original trusses do survive, although they had to be strengthened and repaired in 1736. The main roof trusses have to span about 36 feet (11 m) and the rafters have a pitch of almost 60 degrees. They were given internal strength by having a system of collars and scissor-braces in each truss. These made them very strong and able to support the heavy lead coverings, but their weakness, as Sir Christopher Wren first

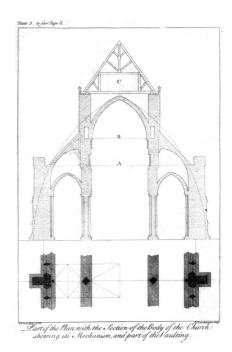

ABOVE: Francis Price's measured section through the cathedral, showing how the large outer buttresses and the flying buttresses (under the triforium roofs) support the high vaults. Note also Price's new high roof for the eastern arm of 1736.

BELOW: One of the original 13th-century roof trusses in the triforium, showing a hidden flying buttress behind.

Set of 53 original choir stalls on the south side
of the choir. The stalls (in the foreground) backed
on to a stone choir screen (see p.61).

pointed out, was in not having longitudinal
strengthening. Despite having stone gables
at the ends, this often caused the roof
trusses to rack (lean over), which led to the
need for major repairs in the seventeenth
and eighteenth centuries. When the eastern
arm's high roofs were made in 1234–5,
they were, however, very impressive, and
would have allowed Bishop Robert and
Elias of Dereham to start to put in hand
the internal decoration and furnishings of
the eastern arm. The ridges of these great
roofs were (and still are) about 115 feet
(35 m) above the ground and, at this time,
the only thing being built that was higher
than this was the lantern tower over the
crossing. Dendrochronology now tells us
that this was probably not finally roofed
until 1242, and this was the one space that
was planned originally not to have a stone
vault over it. The fine lierne vault (pp.90–1
and 107) was not made until 1479–80
(see Chapter 9). We also have no idea of
the form of the original roof covering the
crossing, but it may have been a timber-
and-lead spire.

Another very specific gift from Henry III
was of twenty 'good oaks', given to the
dean and chapter from trees 'scattered
about' in Chippenham Forest 'to make
stalls in their church'. This confirms
Matthew Paris's account of Bishop Robert
completing 'the choir stalls and the lead
roofing of the front of the church'. For
the choir stalls, carefully selected timber
would have to be found, particularly for
the carved elements. Remarkably, almost
all of these wonderful stalls still survive in
the cathedral, although they were extensively restored in the 1870s. With 106 of
them in total, they are the earliest complete
set to survive in Britain. (The smaller set of

Detail of an angel on the c.1236
choir screen, playing the harp.

OPPOSITE: Reconstruction of the choir and presbytery, early 16th-century, showing the stalls of all the principal dignitaries.

BELOW: Remains of the choir screen's west façade now on the north-east transept's west wall. In the centre is the relocated doorway into Bishop Beauchamp's chantry chapel. Note some of the reconstructed grisaille glass in the windows above.

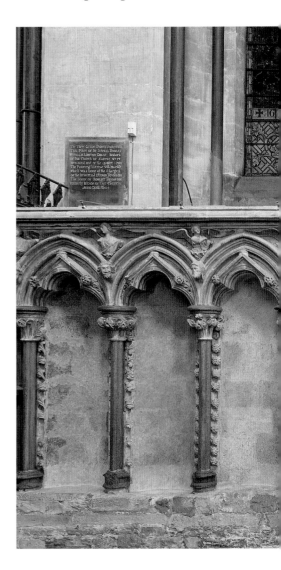

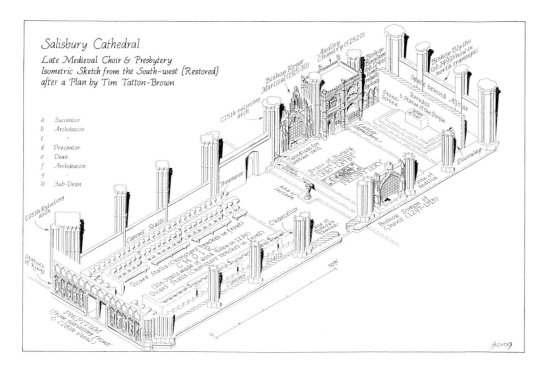

Salisbury Cathedral
Late Medieval Choir & Presbytery
Isometric Sketch from the South~west (Restored)
after a Plan by Tim Tatton~Brown

a   Succentor
b   Archdeacon
c   "
d   Precentor
e   Dean
f   Archdeacon
g   "
h   Sub-Dean

monks' stalls in Rochester Cathedral's choir was made about ten years earlier, but the stalls there have been almost entirely rebuilt.) The Salisbury stalls were made in two rows, set one above the other with return stalls at the west end. They were deliberately made so that each of the four principal dignitaries, the archdeacons and all the 52 canons and their vicars (in the lower stalls) would have his own tip-up seat (misericord) with arm-rests above. This splendid furniture is still very much in use, with the slightly larger seats at the four 'corners' for the treasurer (on the north-east), chancellor (south-east), and the dean and precentor on the west, all of which flank the double-door entry into the choir from the crossing. The one thing that is now missing is the large stone screen, or pulpitum, behind the return stalls at the west end. This must have been made in about 1236 as well, but it was sadly removed in 1789. Luckily the fronts of the two sections of the western face (on either side of the double doorway) were saved, and re-erected against the west wall of the north-east transept. The double doorway itself, which had flat lintels over the openings and was probably made of Purbeck marble, was destroyed, but luckily we have an idea of its form from a drawing of the nave made in 1754 (see p.116).

With the completion of the roofs and high vaults of the eastern arm, scaffolding would have remained in place so that the vaults and the walls could be decorated. Traces of the original painted decoration can still be seen in many places, as can the nineteenth-century repainting of this decoration over the choir. Most splendid of all, however, was the very fine series of painted roundels, which contained different painted schemes covering the high vaults. Unfortunately, these were heavily white-washed over in 1789, and then (aside from the roundels on the transept vaults) were

repainted in the later nineteenth century. Above the eastern crossing, between the choir and presbytery, is a nineteenth-century depiction of Christ in Majesty at the centre of these roundels, surrounded by the evangelists and the apostles. On the choir vaults are the Old Testament prophets, while over the presbytery are the labours of the months. To the north and south of the crossing is the barely visible original painting scheme, which shows a whole series of angels in roundels, holding a mass of different attributes. (See p.6.)

In a similar way, a large number of stained-glass artists were brought in to work alongside the painters, who filled all the lancet window openings with much glorious 'stained' (painted) glass. Even less of this survives than of the wall paintings because it was all mostly destroyed after 1789. However, much recent work by modern scholars of wall-paintings and stained glass has allowed us a better understanding of what was here originally.

All the main decorative work was probably taking place between 1237 and 1243, although we have no direct documentary evidence for this. One tiny clue is the donation by the king again, of gifts of 'logs for making lime' to Elias of Dereham for the 'church of St Mary' from local woods (Bramshaw, Hants and

Repainted roundels, early 1870s, on the eastern crossing vault. Note the larger figure of Christ in Majesty in the centre.

Virgin and Child in the missal of Henry of Chichester. The mid-13th century image was probably painted at Salisbury, and the architectural detailing and decorative style reflect those of the cathedral.

Grovely, north-west of Wilton). Perhaps this was for the large amount of lime used below the decoration. All this work was seen to be to the glory of the Blessed Virgin Mary, whose magnificent new cathedral of Salisbury was at last nearly ready for services in the choir.

The end of all this work was probably reached in 1244, when there are records of the king giving various items for the furnishings. These include a new pyx (container in which wafers for communion are kept) and vestments, including two copes of 'red silk with gold fringes and little bells'. The copes have long gone, but the cathedral still has a magnificent wooden cope chest, which may well have been made at this time.

We have no specific documentary evidence to say when the services started in the choir and presbytery, but it must have been in about 1244–5. We know that, in 1245, 'the incomparable' Elias of Dereham died after 25 years of service at the cathedral, and the following year Bishop Robert also died. It would be nice to think of them, in the last few months of their lives, enjoying the new liturgies of the Sarum Use, which were at last being celebrated in the glorious new space that they had created.

Large wooden cope chest, perhaps dating from 1244, with a later medieval lid.

6

THE COMPLETION OF THE CATHEDRAL

When Bishop Robert de Bingham died on 2 November 1246, Salisbury – and Gothic architecture in England – had reached a new watershed. During that year work had started on Westminster Abbey, a vast building that would benefit from almost unlimited funds from Henry III, who hoped that he would eclipse even the greatest new buildings in the Ile-de-France. In 1246, at Westminster Abbey, the foundations for a new eastern arm were laid out next to the new Lady Chapel. The plan was for a French *chevet* (semicircular ring of five chapels around the ambulatory) with a large double-aisled transept to the west and a monumental doorway into this space from the north. To the south, a large, new octagonal chapter house was started at the same time, which was joined directly to the south-east corner of the transept. Master Henry de Reyns was appointed to manage this work. As 'master of the king's masons' at Windsor Castle in 1243, he had built the magnificent new chapel and cloister there. Although it is not certain whether he was French or English, there is no doubt that he had acquired all the

latest ideas on French Gothic architecture by working in France – almost certainly during the great 1211–41 rebuilding of Rheims Cathedral, the French coronation church.

The year 1246 was the first in which an 'insider' was *not* appointed bishop of Salisbury, and the man chosen was one of the royal justices: William of York. As provost of Beverley Minister as well (Thomas Becket had also been nominally provost there a century before), William had perhaps overseen the large-scale rebuilding of the eastern arm of Beverley Minister for the archbishop of York, Walter de Gray (1216–55). William was also a canon of York, Lincoln and St Paul's in London, so he had probably witnessed most of the great church-building in England at this time, while also acting as an itinerant royal justice.

William of York was elected as bishop of Salisbury at the end of 1246 (Henry III gave his formal assent on 10 December), but it was not until 14 July 1247 that he was consecrated at Wilton Abbey. Soon afterwards he appointed Master Ralph of

York as the *custos fabricæ* (warden of the fabric) of the cathedral (following the death of Elias of Dereham), and gave him the 'golden' prebend of Charminster and Bere, which was the richest prebend of all – worth 80 marks a year. Bishop William also employed another man from the north, Nicholas of York, whom he made canon of Grantham Australis – another rich prebend worth 50 marks. Nicholas is also referred to as 'Li Engingnur', and probably as the *magister operis* (master of the works), so we seem to have new management coming in at this critical time.

As well as the new men from the North, there was some continuity from the past, especially the dean, Robert of Hertford, a former chancellor who became dean in 1236 and died in 1257. However, the precentor, from 1244 to 1270, was the absentee Andrew of Lavagna, a nephew of Pope Innocent IV (1243–54). This pernicious practice of 'papal provisions' was to get more common at the end of the century. Despite this, there was a distinguished resident chancellor, Ralph de Hecham (1241–71), a doctor of theology, who had recently been chancellor of Oxford University, while the treasurer from 1246 was Robert de Cardevill (although he was granted leave to study in Paris, in July 1248). Finally, the archdeacon of Berkshire from 1237, Giles of Bridport, was elected as the next bishop in 1256 (consecrated in 1257), but he died at the end of 1262. He was succeeded by Walter de la Wyle in 1263. From 1248 to 1263 Walter had been the more lowly succentor, but with an absent precentor it was clearly a much more important post.

The main priority in 1247 was to finish the building of the cathedral nave, and most of the main masonry work must have been completed during the following years. Tree-ring samples from the high roof of the nave provide felling dates of 1244 (at the

east end) and 1251. This suggests that the east end of the nave was roofed at exactly the same time as the eastern arm was coming into use. The masons would then have carried on with the building of the rest of the nave before the carpenters returned in about 1252–5. Documentary evidence backs up the tree-ring dating, and the Close Rolls record the donation of gifts

Quadripartite vaults of the nave north aisle looking west from the crossing. Unlike the eastern arm, the decoration of the nave was much more low key, with only red lines being painted on the vault webs – a form of false ashlar. Note, however, the finely carved bosses.

of a whole series of 'good' oaks from the forests of Melksham, Chippenham, Doiley and Finkley (the latter in Chute Forest), between 1251 and 1253. One of the grants even mentions that they were 'for making twenty rafters'. The sixteenth-century historian John Leland records that it was the next bishop, Giles of Bridport, who 'covered the cathedral with lead', but the evidence given above suggests that most of the roof carpentry work was done in the years before Bishop William of York's

death on 31 January 1256. Less than a year before this (on 11 May 1255), the bishop had acquired the rich prebend of Potterne, and this prebend and its stall in the choir have belonged to the bishop (nominally) ever since.

The Salisbury nave, which is 200 feet (60 m) long, is a superb space and, although its lowest walls were built at an early stage, it was only in the late 1240s that it rose to its full height of nearly 90 feet (27 m). In the eastern arm of the

Terry Ball's reconstruction of the cathedral in c.1245, with bells being cast for the new bell-tower and the Bishop's Palace bottom right.

cathedral, the Purbeck marble piers, with their flanking polished shafts, are different in design in each of the different spaces of the cathedral (presbytery, choir, lesser transepts, greater transepts and crossing). Within the nave, they are perhaps at their most majestic, with approximately one-foot-high (30 cm) courses of unpolished drums (cut as a series of blocks to form a quatrefoil, but set diagonally), rising up some 26 feet (7.8 m) to the large polished capitals (see p.41). Above this are the magnificent moulded stone arches (not covered in painted work); the ten bays of the triforium arcades; and the high clerestory's triple openings. On the whole, the nave imparts a feeling of uncluttered purity. The vaults were covered with a simple red-line masonry pattern, with just a little foliage decoration at its highest levels in each bay, much of which was whitewashed over in *c.*1790 (see p.66).

(see p.41)

Clerestories

A careful examination of all the nave's masonry shows that it is not identical to that of the eastern arm, and some subtle changes have occurred. The Purbeck marble shafts in the clerestory of the presbytery, for example, are monolithic shafts (below). Further west, in the large transepts, the shafts are in two sections, with a shaft ring (and a marble-tie to the main wall) in between. By the time the nave was built, the Purbeck marble shaft ring was fixed to the main wall by only an iron tie (below, left).

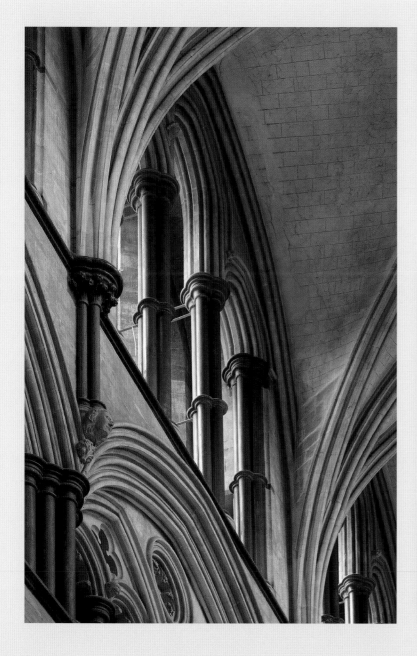

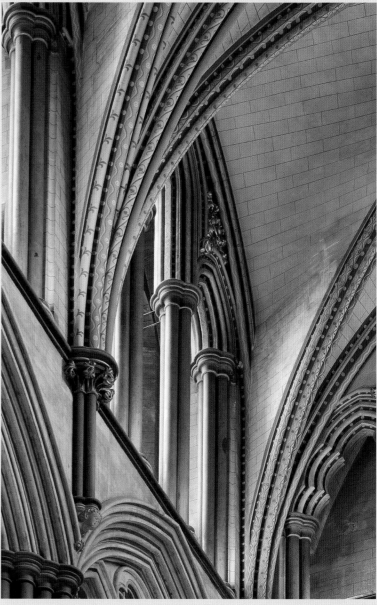

ABOVE: J. M. W. Turner, *North Porch of Salisbury Cathedral*, 1796, watercolour, showing the porch being repaired.

LEFT: The medieval armoire (document cupboard) in the muniment room. The iron hinges and ring handles are original.

One of the other areas of masonry that needed completing in the 1240s was the magnificent north porch. From the outset, this was planned as the principal entrance to the cathedral, but initially a special temporary entrance was created into the north transept, which could be used as the principal entrance into the choir while the nave was being built. Salisbury's north porch is the largest and most imposing of a group of north porches found in the secular cathedrals of south-west England; the others are at Wells, Exeter and Hereford. It is a very tall structure with two bays of rib-vaulting over it and fine blind tracery, although this was quite heavily restored in 1880–1. During this period, the porch's interior was completely renovated and new paving was laid by the architect G. E. Street. Despite this, the detailing of the north porch's architecture suggests a slightly later date than that used in the eastern arm. We find, for example, the first use of cusping in the heads of all the arches (see picture on p.33).

Hidden away behind the south-east corner of the porch is a tiny spiral staircase that leads from the nave to the chamber above the porch (sometimes called the parvise chamber). This fine room, which is now used to hold the cathedral's fabric records, has the most elaborate original roof in the whole cathedral. Not only does it have a series of scissor-braced trusses (braces crossed like scissor blades) but also, to strengthen them longitudinally, are 'crown-posts' and cross-braces, which were most unusual at that time. This roof runs directly into the triforium roof of the north aisles, and recent tree-ring dating has shown that some of the English timbers used here were cut down in the winters of 1251–2 and 1254–6. On top of the roof trusses are rows of small horizontal timbers (known as sarking boards), which are used to support the lead sheets

Internal view of the singers' gallery in the centre of the west front (see p.83).

(see p.83)

The west front was studied in detail during the restoration work of the 1990s, and one major conclusion reached was that only the lowest two levels of the turret-niches, and those on the central buttresses, ever contained sculpture in the Middle Ages. Most of the sculpture on the west front was installed only after the G. G. Scott restoration during the 1870s. Immediately beneath the main triple west window is a level of Victorian figures, which virtually cover a horizontal row of nine quatrefoil openings. Behind these openings is a gallery that was almost certainly used by the singers for the Palm Sunday liturgy. Similar, but smaller, galleries also exist in the west fronts of Wells and Lichfield cathedrals.

BELOW: John Britton's view of the west front in c.1820 before the Victorian statues were added. Note the quatrefoil opening to the singers' gallery in the middle, and the late-medieval crenellated top parapet.

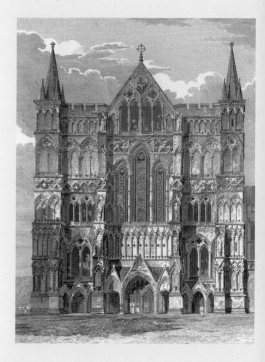

covering the roofs. Amazingly, some of these boards were found to be original ones made with Irish oak, also during the 1250s. When the roof was repaired in 2000, it was discovered that some of the lead sheets on the north-aisle roof had not been replaced since the 1660s. Until the most recent re-roofing work, all the lead would have been taken off the roofs and melted down in the nearby cathedral workshops. The molten lead was then poured on to a sand table to make the new lead sheets. In the most recent re-roofing, for this to be done in accordance with modern Health and Safety Regulations, all the lead had to be taken to a modern 'plumbery' at Leicester and back!

During the later 1240s and early 1250s, by far the finest structure of the cathedral to be completed was the west front. Unlike the great screens or façades that were added on to many Italian cathedrals (often at a later date), Salisbury's west front was built up in a series of stages while the nave was being completed. As a consequence, its windows reflect the inside spaces, as do all its levels. Despite this, the west front was clearly built originally to have three monumental doorways at the base (with gables over them), and above this a large series of fairly shallow niches for statues. In this, it was following the form of the neighbouring cathedral of Wells. But in contrast to Wells, the west front at Salisbury does not incorporate western towers, and it is a much taller and squarer structure. The whole façade is about 110 feet (33 m) square, with its raised 'curtain walls' on either side, but its top is given a strikingly large central gable (on the end of the nave roof) and stone spirelets (on the two outer stair turrets). These are the earliest stone spires to survive here and must have been in place by the later 1250s.

On the south side of the nave, in the outer wall at its west end, it is possible to see that the original doorway opening has been blocked up and replaced by another doorway further to the west (see p.33). This shows that when this part of the nave was being completed, the construction of a larger cloister was already being planned (see p.55). Furthermore, the cloister arcades were to be given traceried openings in the new French Gothic style. This was to be the largest and most spectacular cloister in England and, although it was not completed until *c*.1265, work on its enlargement may have already started in the 1250s.

Two other undocumented buildings must also have been underway at this time: the bell-tower and the two-storey octagonal structure containing the treasury and muniment room (below). The bell-tower,

OPPOSITE: Francis Price's plan, section and elevation of the bell-tower, made in 1746 not long before its demolition. His design for a new domed belfry was never made.

The muniment room (above) and the treasury (below), which were added to the cathedral by *c*.1250. Note how the lower windows were heavily barred, with the outer bars now removed. Until 1790 another building (which stood in the foreground) abutted the treasury.

A Section and Plan of the Belfry: with a Scheme for a Roof, when the Spire stands in need of being renewed.

which was about 200 feet (60 m) due north of the north porch, was a massive buttressed masonry structure about 50 feet (15 m) square and 80 feet (24 m) high. Most unfortunately, it was completely demolished in 1790 and its site is now only revealed by a large summer parch-mark in the grass of the northern churchyard. Fortunately, there are various earlier views of it, as well as a fine plan, elevation and section (by Francis Price, left). On top of the masonry tower was a large timber-framed and lead-covered belfry, with a magnificent timber-and-lead spire above, whose apex was about 200 feet above the ground. The belfry contained not only a fine set of bells (which must have been cast originally in the churchyard below) but also, from the later fourteenth century, what is probably the earliest surviving clock in England.

England's earliest clock

First documented in 1386, in 1790 this clock was moved to the crossing tower on the cathedral, where it was replaced in 1884 by a fine new Victorian clock. In 1955 the medieval original was taken down, restored and placed on display in the nave's north aisle.

The restored 14th-century clock, with the striking mechanism on the right.

The treasury and muniment room building is the one edifice adjacent to the cathedral that was an after-thought. It abuts the south-east side of the south-east transept, and one can see how the south wall of the southern chapel in the transept has been cut through to make the entry into the vestibule. Externally, the vestibule walls butt up against the main buttresses here. A treasury and muniment room would have been required as soon as the eastern arm of the cathedral came into use, so it is very likely that this building was put up between *c.*1240 and 1250. Its octagonal form mirrors the nearby chapter house, so the two buildings may have been planned at the same time, though no other dating evidence is yet available. Unlike the chapter house, however, the treasury building was made to be a very strong repository of the cathedral's treasure and records. Therefore it has very small windows that are heavily barred; in fact, the lower windows had double sets of bars, although the outer ones are now gone.

The vestibule of the treasury was reached from the cathedral through the original double doors, and there was a second pair of doors into the treasury itself. On the west side of the vestibule, another lockable door leads to a stone staircase in the thickness of the wall, which gives access through two further doors to the muniment room above. This also has small barred windows with internal wooden shutters. In the east wall of the treasury and of the muniment room above are blocked up doorways that, before 1790, led to a small rectangular extension to the building. This almost certainly contained the sub-treasurer's chambers, because all the wooden doors mentioned above could only be bolted or locked from the inside; so this would have been done by a man, who presumably locked himself in for the night. In the vestibule, in the east wall, is an

Early 19th-century muniment room (from 1970,
the choir practice room). It contained all the
cathedral's archives (including Magna Carta), most
of which were in locked iron-bound chests.

original fireplace (and chimney flue above)
– the only thirteenth-century one in the
whole cathedral complex. Nearby was a
beautiful carved *lavatorium* (wash basin),
which the canons could use to keep warm
in the winter and wash their hands before
going into the choir for a service. A
thirteenth- to fourteenth-century fireplace
and *lavatorium* can still be seen in the
vestry at Lincoln Minster. The first-floor
muniment room at Salisbury was still in
use for its original purpose as late as 1970,
but in that year all the large muniment
chests were removed and put in the
presbytery aisles of the cathedral, so that
the room could become the choir practice
room. Luckily we have an early nineteenth-
century drawing showing the room still
in use as originally intended (see above).
Along one of the walls is a very fine
muniment cupboard, or armoire, in which
Salisbury's Magna Carta and the Chapter
Act Books were formerly kept. The
original glazed tile floor of the muniment
room survives on a timber floor, although
it is now mostly covered up. Sadly, all
the ancient timberwork of the floor and
roof was replaced in 1932 with replica
new timbers.

Perhaps the most remarkable additional
building that was created adjacent to the
cathedral was the chapter house. Most
unusually for the Middle Ages, this was
a near copy of the new royal chapter house
at Westminster Abbey, which was nearing
completion in 1253 and was described by
Matthew Paris as a 'chapter house beyond

The decorated 14th-century *lavatorium* now in
the north-east transept, but formerly outside the
outer vestry in the south-east transept.

Chapter house on the east side of the cloister, with its large traceried windows in the new 'Westminster Abbey' style.

compare'. A polygonal chapter house had recently been built at Lincoln Minster, as well as at Beverley Minster, William of York's former church. The Beverley chapter house has since been destroyed, but in the north choir aisle there, it is still possible to see the very striking double staircase leading up to its vestibule. As at Westminster (and later Wells Cathedral), the Beverley chapter house was built on an undercroft. This was unnecessary at Salisbury because the smaller octagonal building for the treasury and muniments had already been built further to the east. It seems likely that Bishop William and senior members of the chapter saw the Westminster chapter house in the early 1250s, and decided that he would have a building of exactly the same form and size at Salisbury. However, he improved on the Westminster design by having far more elegant blind arcading in the lower wall above the benching, and above this a superb frieze was carved, which depicts the principal scenes in the first two books of the Bible, starting on the north-west with the Creation and ending on the south-west with Moses receiving the Tablets of the Law. In between are scenes showing the building of Noah's Ark, the destruction of Sodom and Gomorrah, and Moses and the Burning Bush. The sculpture was damaged in the mid-seventeenth century, but was well restored in 1855, when the new carved heads of Caen stone were pieced in to replace the lost ones. Most of the Purbeck marble was also replaced at this time. As at Westminster, the seats against the east wall (for the principal persons) were raised up a step and set back further into the wall. However, the Westminster Abbey chapter house only has five seats per bay, whereas at Salisbury, it was seven seats per bay, making 51 seats in all – enough to take the bishop and whole chapter. The seven most important seats in the east wall were probably used by the bishop, dean, precentor and the four archdeacons. The two slightly larger seats on the west (on either side of the double doorway) were perhaps used by the chancellor and treasurer, which would have reflected the 'four-square' seating in the choir.

Bishop William of York died on 31 January 1256, and in his place Giles of Bridport, the dean of Wells, was quickly elected bishop by the canons; this was accepted by Henry III, as Matthew Paris tells us. However, the process was then held up in June, when the king sent the bishop-elect and the abbot of Westminster (Richard Crokesley) on a secret mission (concerning the 'Sicilian Affair') to Pope Alexander IV in Rome. The new bishop was now involved in the chaotic papal affairs in the 'Eternal City', for several months, before returning to England over the Alps and through 'hostile' France early in 1257. No doubt, to his great relief, he was consecrated bishop of Salisbury in Canterbury Cathedral by Archbishop Boniface on 11 March 1257, although he annoyed the chapter at Wells by claiming that the pope had given him letters that allowed him to remain as dean of Wells as well!

When Bishop Giles finally arrived back in Salisbury to be enthroned on 1 April, he would have seen that all the masonry of the cathedral had been completed, and his one major contribution to the work (as Leland tells us) was to provide the final ingots of lead (perhaps from the Mendips, near Wells) to complete the nave roof. A statute, concerning church consecrations (promulgated at a council held at St Paul's Cathedral in 1237), said that all cathedrals and monastic churches or parish churches 'whose walls have been completed must be consecrated within two years of that time'. The bishop thus set about planning a great ceremony of dedication for the

cathedral, which would take place at Michaelmas in 1258. This would have been widely announced, and on 21 May 1258 Pope Alexander issued a decree giving indulgences to penitents and confessors who would visit the 'newly constructed' cathedral on any of the feasts of the Virgin Mary.

The Building of the Tower of Babel and God and Noah, two of the many lively scenes in the chapter house frieze.

This great ceremony duly took place on Sunday 29 September 1258 in the presence of almost all of England's most important figures. These included King Henry III and Queen Eleanor (of Provence), and their two sons, Edward and Edmund, the former with his fourteen-year-old wife, Eleanor of Castile, whom he married in Burgos in October 1254. They had all travelled the three miles from Clarendon Palace accompanied by a large number of barons, who effectively now ruled the kingdom, after a traumatic few months for the king. As well as this, Boniface of Savoy, the archbishop of Canterbury (who was also the queen's uncle), officiated at the ceremony, accompanied by Bishop Giles and at least nine other bishops from England and Wales. Then there was Master Robert de Wickhampton, a papal chaplain, who had recently become dean, and, no doubt, most of the 40 or so canons. Many other lesser members of the clergy would also have attended, as well as many citizens of the new city of Salisbury, including, most certainly, many of the men who had helped to build this superb new cathedral.

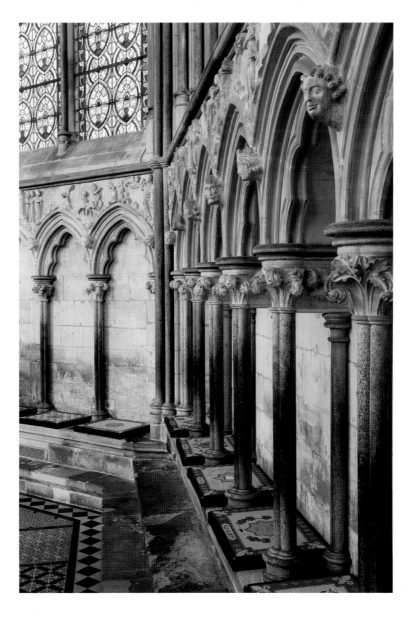

Some of the principal seats in alcoves along the east wall of the chapter house.

7

THE CHAPTER HOUSE AND CLOISTER

With the consecration of the cathedral, the work on this magnificent new building was finally complete, after 40 years of continuous work. Bishop Giles was obviously very pleased with the splendid new setting for his *cathedra*, and in his statutes he proudly declares:

> Whereas among the churches of the whole world, the church of Salisbury shines like the sun in the full orb of its strength, in respect of its divine service and ministries, so far that she sheds her beams on every side and so corrects the shortcomings of other churches.

It is important to remember that the cathedral would have been used continuously from about 1244 for the Sarum Use. Around fifteen years later, the processions on great feast days would have been able to go down the full length of the nave before passing through the gap in the arcade benching, just before the west doors. The nave must have looked spectacular with all its newly painted red-line decoration on the walls and vaults, and with the light coming in through the glorious painted grisaille glass, which filled the huge double lancets on either side. Almost all of this painted glass has gone, but Charles Winston's fine watercolour paintings of the mid-nineteenth century provide a good impression of it, as do the few reconstructed fragments that are now visible in the building.

PLATE, 1.

LEFT: One bay of the cloister arcading, restored in the late 20th century. Until the mid-17th century, all the openings down to the iron bar were glazed.

RIGHT: Charles Winston's 1849 watercolour drawings of some of the grisaille glass from Salisbury Cathedral.

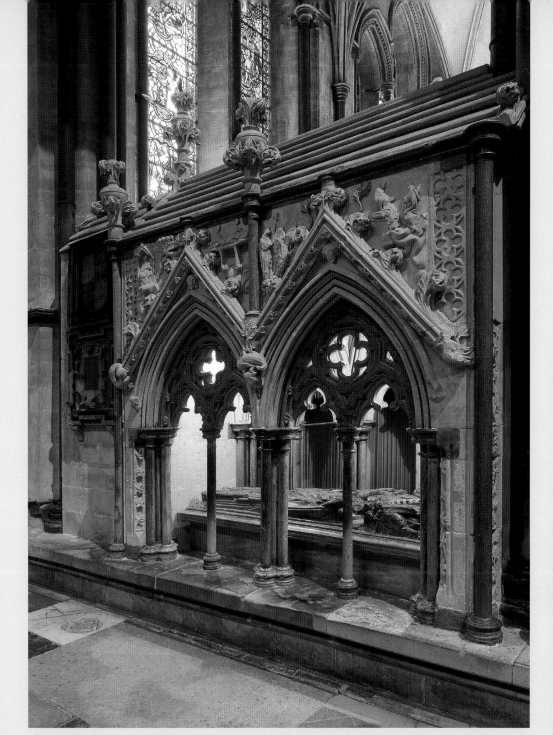

BELOW: Detail of Bishop Giles of Bridport's effigy.

Bishop Giles of Bridport's tomb

This is the finest medieval tomb in the cathedral and, architecturally, it reflects perfectly all that was happening at the cathedral during Bishop Giles' time. The stone coffin lies on the arcade bench covered by a finely carved Purbeck marble effigy of the bishop. Above this is an elaborately carved and extremely handsome gabled monument, which also acts as an open screen between the aisle and the chapel. It is constructed with Tisbury stone and Purbeck marble, and the architectural carving is in the new 'Westminster Abbey' style that was being used at the chapter house. The Purbeck marble cusped openings, with quatrefoils above, are particularly fine and display the excellent skills of the marblers working in Salisbury during this time. Even more extraordinary are the sequence of eight narrative scenes carved on the spandrel panels above the openwork. These are unique and seem to depict scenes in the life of Bishop Giles as if he were a holy man. They were probably carved by some of the skilled mason-carvers who had recently finished the large sequence of similar panels in the chapter house. Much other intricate decorative work was also used on the tomb, and the whole is covered with a sloping 'roof' and a series of finials, some of which are now missing. Note how the monument was extensively defaced, probably in the 17th century, and, unlike the chapter house frieze, has not been restored.

Early 19th-century engraving of De Vaux College from the south. Sadly, soon after this the building was very heavily rebuilt.

The cloister facing north-west, which was used as a prison in the 1650s. Note the west end of the nave behind it, and the cedar tree that was planted in 1837.

Bishop Giles continued to be involved with national affairs and his diocesan duties. However, he was doubtless impatient to see the completion of the new chapter house, and it is likely that work on this continued rapidly after 1258. Bishop Giles also created a new college for two chaplains

and twenty 'poor, needy, honest and teachable' scholars, who were under the warden (a cathedral canon) to study theology and the liberal arts. He put up a large new masonry hall and chapel building for them in the southern part of the Close, which later acquired the name of De Vaux College. In Latin it was called the *domus de valle scholarium*, meaning 'the house of the valley scholars'. Something of the building still survives just outside the late medieval Harnham Gate and close to Bishop Robert's great bridge over the river. In January and July 1261, eighteen more oaks 'fit for timber' were given to Master Ralph of York, who was now the *custos operacionum* (head of works). Gifts from the king, these oaks came from Buckholt and Melchet woods

in Clarendon Forest, and from the bishop of Winchester's wood at Downton; they were perhaps used for the roofs of the chapter house and De Vaux College.

On 13 December 1262, Bishop Giles died and a fine tomb was made for him on the bench between the south choir aisle and the chapel of St Mary Magdalen in the south-east transept where his chantry was created. Soon after his death, the succentor, Walter de la Wyle, was elected bishop. He had been filling in for the absent precentor for over fifteen years and was obviously a highly respected figure. He professed obedience to Archbishop Boniface and was consecrated in Canterbury Cathedral on 27 May 1263. Just over two weeks later,

on 15 June, he formally granted a plot of the bishop's land sixteen feet (4.8 m) wide 'along the length and square of the south side of the cloister, which adjoins our house' (in other words, the bishop's palace, which is now Salisbury Cathedral School). This extra piece of land was needed to enlarge the cloister on the south (having already been enlarged on the west), and to create a new south cloister walk 190 feet (57 m) long. Bishop Walter also specified that he should have a small door from his house into this new cloister walk, so that he had his own 'private' way through the cloister into the cathedral. This doorway was used by successive bishops until 1947, when they stopped living in the

OPPOSITE: West end of the nave, showing the original west doors (with their lattice frames). Above them is the singers' gallery (see p.70), and at the base of the west window can be seen the mid-13th century stained-glass shields from the chapter house (see p.85).

Chapter house vestibule with some original decoration on the vaults.

palace, and it is still used daily by members of the cathedral choir.

The new cloister at Salisbury Cathedral is an exceptionally large and splendid structure, and it is most likely that large quantities of new Tisbury stone and Purbeck marble were brought in to complete its construction over the next few years. The work must have continued rapidly and, for the first time in the cathedral's construction, we find that the mostly hidden outer wall faces on the north and south sides were not made with ashlar masonry but with rubble-work. Between the nave and the north side of the cloister, where early workshops had stood, a sort of 'dead space' was now created, which could only have been entered originally from a doorway cut through the west wall of the south transept. Later this space was used for cathedral workshops, and by the nineteenth century two further doorways were made into it from the south and west. Named the 'plumbery', a term for the workshops used by the lead workers, it is now a very fine space for the cathedral's shop and refectory.

The chapter house and the huge new cloister were almost certainly finished by March 1266, because there is an early fourteenth-century note in the chapter archives that states:

> The church of Sarum was commenced building in the time of King Richard, and continued through the reign of three kings, and was completed on 25 March in the year 1266, the whole expense of the fabric up to that time having been 42,000 marks.

This sum, which translates as £28,000 (a mark is two thirds of a pound), is many millions of pounds at today's values. Moreover, most of the materials would have been 'free', so the real costs were in transportation and in paying for the vast numbers of craftsmen and labourers. There were no management fees, in modern terms, because the project was run by the bishop, dean and canons, all of whom received incomes from their own prebends.

John Britton's 1820 engraving of the chapter house, showing the heraldic shields still *in situ* in the east window.

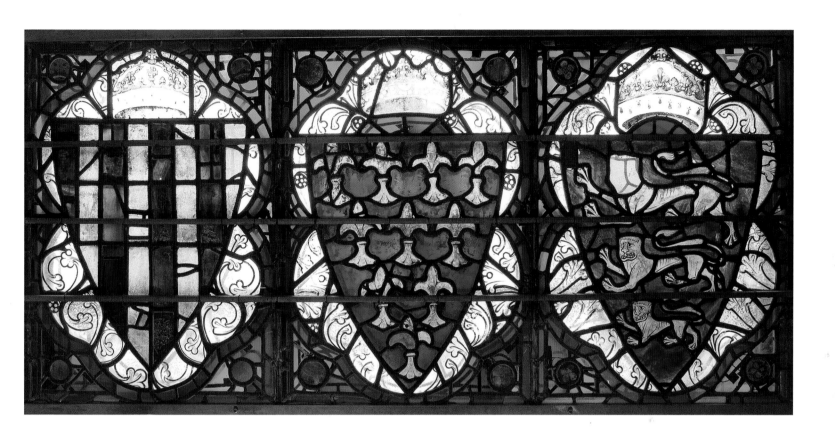

Three of the stained-glass shields from the chapter house, now at the bottom of the central west window (see p.83). They are (from left to right) the arms of Provence, France and England 'ancient'.

When the Salisbury chapter house was finished, its large windows were filled with magnificent stained glass. Most unfortunately, though, the last of these windows (on the east side) was removed in 1821. In the four lower windows were eight shields that ran across the upper part of the grisaille glass. These were immediately above the seven most important seats in the east wall, and luckily some sketch drawings were made of the glass *in situ* before its removal to the bases of the three great lancets in the west wall of the nave. One shield has disappeared and another is restored; despite this, we know that the chapter house shields were for Henry III, Louis IX of France (his brother-in-law),

Queen Eleanor of Provence and Henry III's brother Richard, earl of Cornwall, who had become 'king of the Romans' in 1257.

As well as this, there were the arms of two very powerful nobles: Gilbert de Clare and Roger Bigod, earl of Norfolk, and the now missing shield was almost certainly that of the Lord Edward, the future King Edward I, who was now a key figure in England. It is worth noting that heraldry was new at this time, but similar carved heraldic shields had just been put in the lower walls of the new choir aisles at Westminster Abbey. When all of this work at the abbey came to a temporary end, with the translation of the body of St Edward the Confessor to a new shrine on 13 October 1269, King Henry III had probably spent about £50,000 on the building, a truly enormous sum. However, unlike at Salisbury, the work was far from complete, and his reign was now drawing to a rather sad end after more than half a century.

Just before these final building projects were being completed at Salisbury, England was in turmoil. Henry III had lost everything after being defeated by Simon de Montfort at the Battle of Lewes in 1264, but then all was reclaimed the following year in the great slaughter of the Battle of Evesham on 4 August 1265. Much unrest continued for several years, though the wise counsels of a new papal legate, Ottobuono (later to become Pope Adrian V) – who was in England from 1266 to 1268 – helped calm things down.

One remarkable document survives from this time, which describes the difficult situation in Salisbury. It is a mandate to the dean and chapter of Salisbury from Bishop Walter, and is dated 21 March 1269. In Professor Brian Kemp's summary, it tells us that:

> ... the bishop, having heard that, during the recent troubles, a band of nobles has come to their cloister several times – often with arms – and has pillaged, committed other outrages and, under the pretext of military privilege, trampled under foot the honour due to the nobility (not entirely without the connivance of some of the chapter who have not so far confronted this evil as they ought), has interrupted divine service, and despised and molested the ministers of the cathedral, to the peril of their own soul and the scandal of many – that they (the dean and chapter) are to observe the statutes published by Ottobuono, cardinal deacon of St Adrian and lately legate of the apostolic see, which provide a remedy in this case, by refusing hospitality or admittance to any knights and their entourages who may in the future come to the Close to hold a tournament or other assembly, however it be described, and, if in the future any be admitted or violently invade the Close, they and those who admitted them are to be punished by ecclesiastical censure, and the dean and chapter are to impose, or cause to be imposed on the bishop's behalf, an interdict on the cathedral and on all the churches of the city and diocese up to a five-mile radius until the offenders withdraw and make adequate satisfaction.

Law and order were gradually being restored at this time, and it is interesting to note that the first use by men other than the canons of the chapter house was probably on 16 November 1270 (the feast day of St Edmund of Abingdon, the cathedral's former treasurer who was canonised in 1246), when men from Wiltshire came there to swear an oath of fealty to the Lord Edward and his eldest son, John of Windsor (aged four). By this time Salisbury had become a large city (the tenth largest in England by the early fourteenth century), and much of the northern area of the city had been filled with new houses. To look after their souls and their welfare, Bishop Walter founded a new college in the city in 1269, which was dedicated to St Edmund of Abingdon. It was to consist of a provost and thirteen priests living communally next to the new parish church of St Edmund, who would serve the parish and carry out the college work. They were also expected to attend the great processions in the cathedral, 'weather permitting'.

All work on the cathedral, chapter house and cloister must have been completed by 1269, but there is one interesting gift, recorded in the Close Rolls that year,

BELOW AND OPPOSITE: Some of the many fine carved heads from the chapter house.

of 'ten oaks for joists within the tower of Salisbury from Bedwyn Wood in Savernake Forest'. This may refer to the great freestanding bell-tower in the Close,

and could suggest that the large timber-framed belfry and spire was still being built at this time. Two years later (in 1271), the canon treasurer, Nicholas Longespée (a future bishop), was also given 'ten oaks suitable for timber from Bedwyn Brail'. By this time Bishop Walter had died (on 4 January 1271) and was in the process of being succeeded by the dean, Robert de Wickhampton, who was succeeded as dean by another scholar, Walter Scammel. It is remarkable that all three of Bishop Walter's successors had previously been dean. This shows that, by the later thirteenth century, Salisbury was a very powerful and independent body, with most of its bishops (and deans) deriving from the chapter itself. With its great wealth and, no doubt, the prestige of its glorious new cathedral, the chapter also contained many royal clerks; so its connections with the Crown were also close. By the later thirteenth century, there were at least a dozen canons' houses in the Close, and Dean Robert de Wickhampton was living in an elegant large house opposite the west front. After he became bishop, he formally handed over this house to the chapter in 1277 as the future residence for all deans; it remained in use by them until 1922.

By the end of the thirteenth century, the town and Close had reached a high watermark and both were very prosperous. They were ruled by Bishop Nicholas Longespée, the son of the respected Earl William Longespée, the first person to be buried in the new cathedral some 70 years earlier. Bishop Nicholas died on 18 May 1297, followed only three weeks later by Dean Simon de Mitcham, and then less than a year after that by the precentor, William of Abingdon. Things were to change but, as shown in the next chapter, two great scholar-bishops were to come to Salisbury and erect its greatest glory: the immense tower and spire.

8

BUILDING THE TOWER AND SPIRE

The year 1297 was a momentous one for Salisbury. King Edward I was at the high point of his reign, having recently conquered Wales and Scotland, but in January 1297 the clergy, led by Archbishop Robert Winchelsea, refused to pay the tax levied on it for the king's new war in France. Edward I was furious, outlawed the clergy and sent in royal agents to seize the ecclesiastical estates. He also summoned his magnates to a parliament at Salisbury, to discuss his military plans. The king arrived at Clarendon Palace in late February, and Parliament gathered (perhaps in the chapter house, but without the bishops or clergy) at the beginning of

March. At this meeting the king's chief magnates refused to go with him to Gascony, which once again enraged him. By this time Bishop Nicholas Longespée and many of the clergy had submitted (and paid the fine) to the king, but Parliament dispersed in chaos, and two months later Salisbury was left leaderless when both the bishop and dean died. Archbishop Winchelsea, however, quickly ensured that his friend and ally, Simon of Ghent, was elected bishop of Salisbury by the chapter. Then, on 31 July 1297, as the king left London for Flanders, the clergy had their estates restored and the king gave his assent to the election of Simon as bishop.

LEFT: The huge early 14th-century timber-frame in the spire, which was built as a scaffold during its construction.

RIGHT: Bishop Simon of Ghent's tomb on the south side of the presbytery. Note the use of ballflower on the left and right jambs, and the fleuron-trail on the underside of the ogee arch over the contemporary iron grating.

The new dean, however, was to be Peter of Savoy, a kinsman of the king, who went to Rome in April 1298 and never returned. He was replaced as dean by a French cardinal.

The new bishop, Simon of Ghent, was a very distinguished Oxford scholar; he had been archdeacon of Oxford, a regent doctor of theology and chancellor of the university in 1291–3 (a few years after Robert Winchelsea). After his consecration in Canterbury Cathedral on 20 October 1297, Bishop Simon proved himself to be a very conscientious diocesan bishop, who also worked closely with the archbishop. Bishop Simon complained to Pope Boniface VIII about the pope's appointing of outsiders as dignitaries and prebends of his cathedral, and fought hard to make his canons (particularly the royal clerks) keep their periods of residence at the cathedral. He also did much to educate his clergy and allowed leave of absence for them to study at the universities (particularly at Oxford, but also at Cambridge, Paris and Orleans). He also ensured that theological lectures were given in the cathedral, and in 1314 he had the song school in the Close properly endowed for a grammar master and fourteen choristers. Bishop Simon also had to undertake some work for the king, which included going to France on a peace mission in 1299. Also, after a long dispute with the citizens of Salisbury in 1302–6, he obtained his tallage (a local tax) from them and used that to fund the building of a new guildhall in the marketplace.

By the early fourteenth century, some quite remarkable buildings were being erected in England, including the splendid octagon and lantern over the monks' choir at Ely Cathedral and the new Lady Chapel there; the new eastern arm at St Augustine's Abbey Church in Bristol (now a cathedral); and the Lady Chapel at Wells Cathedral. These were all 'virtuoso'

works, which were being built at a high point in English architecture, a period when some technically daring structures were being constructed in timber (with a covering in lead) and stone. The greatest patrons for these projects were the senior churchmen. Despite the wars in Scotland and the difficulties at Court after the accession of King Edward II in 1307, most great cathedrals and abbeys in England were building something new in the early fourteenth century. At Salisbury the documentary evidence is unfortunately missing, but it seems very likely that it was Bishop Simon who started to build the new tower, shortly before his death on 3 April 1315. In doing this he was following many of the other secular cathedrals in England (Lincoln, Wells, Lichfield, Hereford and St Paul's in London), and one of the most impressive features of early fourteenth-century building work was the use of a decorative element now known as 'ballflower'.

Ballflower
A ballflower is a small ornament carved like an opening bud with several petals, which covers all the jambs, tracery and pinnacles of the moulded surface. Literally thousands of ballflowers were carved, which must have been a very time-consuming job for many masons. This would not have been possible after the huge depopulation caused by the Black Death in 1348–50.

OPPOSITE: Lierne vault put over the crossing in 1479–80.

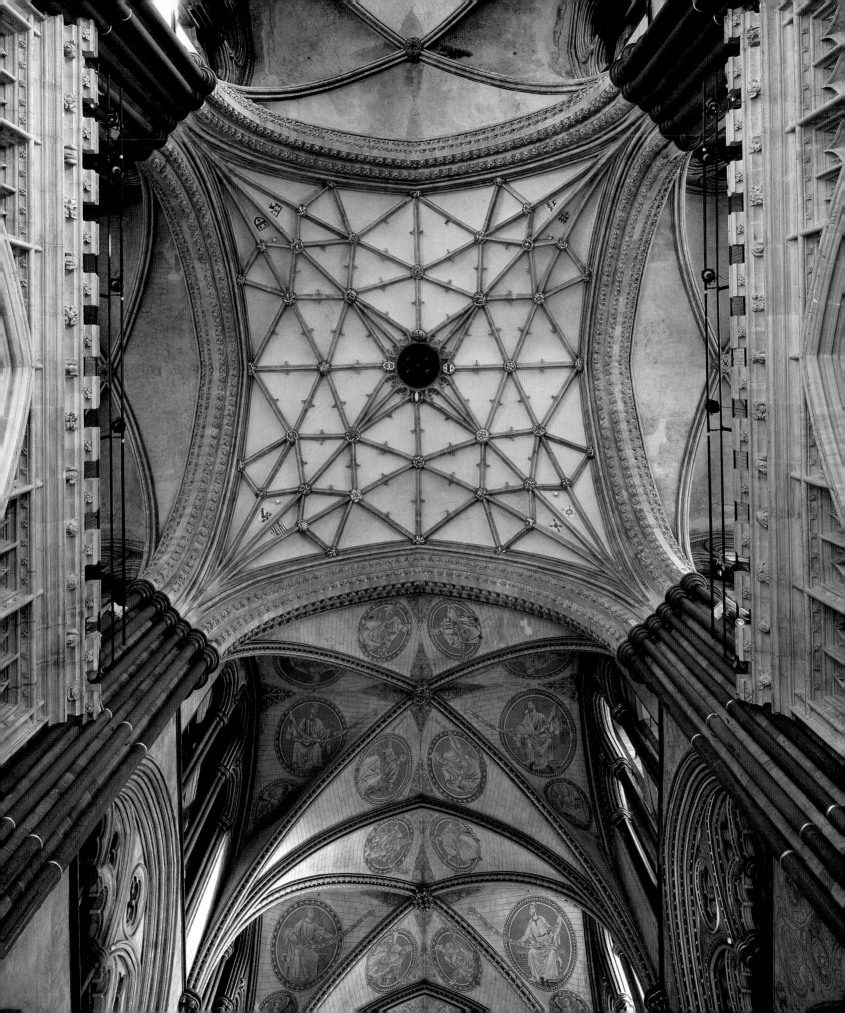

Perhaps shortly after 1310, the existing roof over the lantern tower above the crossing (probably a timber-and-lead spire) was dismantled and a new scaffold was erected above the main high roofs around the outside of the tower. The high ceiling timber-trusses above the lantern were then lowered to the main vault level as a floor, to make a working platform for the new work and to seal off the building site from the crossing below. With this new platform in place, the areas behind the Purbeck marble piers on the inside of the lantern could be filled up to thicken and strengthen the lower tower walls. Before this was done, a wall-passage was created around the inside of the lantern, which connected the eight doors inside the high roof spaces to the spiral stairs in the four corners of the tower. In these passages the outer wall of the tower was only about two feet (60 cm) thick.

OPPOSITE: Upper part of the tower and the spire from the north-east.

BELOW LEFT: Drawn plan and sections of the tower, showing the many inserted structural features.

BELOW: Detail of the lowest part of the tower, showing both ballflower decoration and ballflower joined with fleuron-trails. Note also the crenellated 'parapet'.

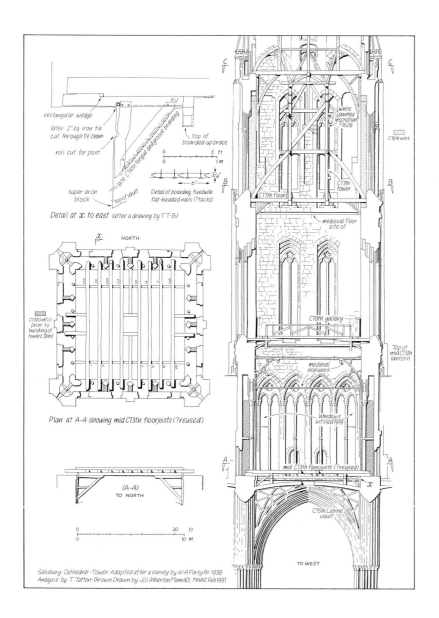

At this initial stage of the work, a substantial new upper stage to the tower was clearly being planned, but nothing as huge as the final 265-foot-high (81 m) masonry tower and spire. The evidence for this is in the very lowest part of the new work, where a crenellated (fortified) parapet and, below it, a string-course of ballflower with water-spouts in it runs all the way around the outside of the tower, joined together by a fleuron-trail (ornamental termination at the edge of a roof). Normally, a parapet would appear at the top of a structure, but here it is at the base of the tower, an indication that perhaps originally nothing was conceived beyond the tower parapet. A very similar fleuron-trail can be seen on the ogee arch over Bishop Simon's tomb (see p.89) on the south side of the presbytery in the cathedral, which must have been made soon after his death on 2 April 1315, at his London house, next to St Bride's church, Fleet Street. Like several bishops at this time, Bishop Simon was considered to be of exceptional holiness (as well as of great learning), and miracles were soon being reported at his tomb. However, unlike Bishop Thomas Cantilupe of Hereford, who was canonised in 1320, no further action was taken here.

Bishop Simon's successor was his friend Master Roger Martival, who had succeeded him at Oxford as chancellor of the university in 1293. A decade earlier Roger had been studying at the University of Paris and, like Simon of Ghent, was clearly a very considerable scholar. He resigned the chancellorship at Oxford in 1295 on becoming archdeacon of Leicester and, in 1298, was given the prebend of Netheravon in Salisbury Cathedral by Bishop Simon. In 1306–7 we know Roger travelled to the Papal Court (on Lincoln chapter business), and in 1310 he was made dean of Lincoln at exactly the same time that the upper part of the crossing tower at Lincoln was being built. It seems very likely that Dean Roger oversaw the building of the very large timber-and-lead spire on top of the tower, which, like that of Old St Paul's Cathedral, reached a height of at least 450 feet (137 m). After being elected bishop of Salisbury on 11 June 1315, he was probably shown the uncompleted crossing tower, but soon afterwards decided not only to make a much higher tower but also to have a large stone spire on top of it. It is worth noting that this was an age of stone spire building, and some of the tallest spires were erected on the parish churches belonging to the cathedrals. Notable examples of major stone spires at Salisbury prebends are those at Grantham (272 feet / 83 m high) in Lincolnshire, and at St Mary Redcliffe (292 feet / 89 m) outside Bristol. It is also surely no coincidence that the University Church in Oxford has a near-contemporary stone spire that is a less accomplished 'prototype' for the Salisbury spire.

At the level of the new work at the top of the lantern tower, mentioned above, it is possible to see that a very elaborate series of iron tie-bars (at two levels) were put in to bind up the critical area at the base of the new tower. These long iron bars run through the masonry walls (where they were set in lead) to external tie-bars, while inside they are joined together by elaborate braces and ties, which in places have decorated ogee elements. This is the most elaborate example of medieval structural ironwork known in Britain.

Above the ironwork, two stages of the new masonry tower were then built some 80 feet (24 m) high. Internally all the masonry is of plain ashlar, with parts of the masonry in the upper chamber being 'thinned down' to reduce the weight and quantity of stone used. Externally, however, much elegantly carved masonry in the Decorated style is used. Once again all the jambs, mullions and pilasters, among other things, are covered in carved ballflower work.

OPPOSITE: Tower and spire, seen from the Bishop's Garden (see also John Constable's depiction of this scene on p.113).

Detail of early 14th-century bars (with a forelock bolt), showing how they run through a plate-tracery opening in the 13th-century lantern tower.

Elaborate early 14th-century iron tie-bars at the top of the lantern tower. The thicker diagonal tie-bars beneath were put in for G. G. Scott in the 1860s.

As soon as the top of the upper stage of the new tower was reached, four diagonal arches were made on the inside (technically known as squinch arches) to form the supports for the stone spire. The octagonal base for the spire was then made on the central parts of the inner half of the tower walls. In the middle of each face, a pair of doors was created that led to external parapet walks, each with an elaborately decorated balustrade on the outside. At one end of each parapet walk, a small doorway leads to the top of a spiral staircase in each of the corner turrets. These turrets are capped by seven-sided spirelets with tall pinnacles (all covered in ballflower) behind them, which sit on the broaches of the spire above the squinch arches. All of this masonry gives added weight and strength to the base of the spire.

The tower was clearly built with external and internal wooden scaffolding, as one can see from the putlog holes. To build the spire, however, only an internal scaffold was used, and amazingly the main frame for this still survives within the spire because, at its apex, it was joined to a vertical iron bar that ran on up through the capstones to an iron cross, and had additional iron ties into the masonry below. Once these were made, the top of the spire was 'locked up' and the timber scaffold became a 'dead weight' inside the spire, suspended from the ironwork, which gave it added stability. Sadly, the ironwork at the top of the spire, as well as the masonry here, were all removed in 1950 and replaced by a new bronze vertical tie-bar, set in new Clipsham stone masonry. The rest of the spire walls – which are only five inches (13 cm) thick in areas where there is an external decorative band – are still made with the original Tisbury stone masonry. Each block in the spire wall is joined to its neighbour both horizontally and vertically with iron cramps set in lead, and the whole structure at the top of the highest capstone, is just over 180 feet (55 m) high, making the iron cross on top a little over 400 feet (122 m) above the ground. Salisbury is thus by far the tallest medieval masonry building in Britain.

To build the spire a very carefully drawn, full-size half-section plan of the whole spire would have been made, to allow each ring of masonry to be very accurately cut on the ground. This was perhaps done on a plaster tracing surface on the nave floor, which is 200 feet (61 m) long. The idea for this suggestion comes from an accurately drawn cross-section of the top part of the spire on the north aisle wall. With all the spire masonry being cut in advance on the ground, it would have taken only a short time (perhaps just a few years) to build the spire, and it is likely that the people of Salisbury first saw their new spire nearing completion in the early 1320s.

During this time, the large extra weight of the tower and spire were forcing the four crossing piers and their adjoining masonry further downwards into the foundations, as can still be seen today. Luckily the still slightly 'plastic' lime mortar allowed this to happen, and the settlement of all the piers was fairly uniform, although there is now a slight lean of just over two feet (60 cm) to the south-west. Bishop Roger's masons were, however, undaunted by the settlement and the appearance of some cracks in the thirteenth-century walls.

A whole series of flying buttresses were constructed internally and externally around the base of the tower in the triforium and clerestory levels (see pp.53 and 99). Most of these have mouldings on them of an early fourteenth-century date. Some of them, including flying buttresses over the nave aisles and eastern

arm roofs, are dated to the later medieval period, and show that differential settlement continued for some time. By the seventeenth century at the latest, the whole structure had finally stabilised, and this is still the case today, although the cathedral's consulting engineer has to make regular checks on its stability.

While this extraordinary structure was being erected, Bishop Roger was working very hard at his cathedral and in his large diocese to bring discipline to the cathedral chapter (and other clergy). Many more of the canons were non-resident and were being provided by the pope; this applied particularly to the major dignitaries (especially the dean). The bishop and the resident canons made many strong protests, mostly to no avail, and on one occasion they famously declared that the 'dignitaries were meant to be like the living cornerstones or pillars of the cathedral, and their neglect of residence might cause the whole fabric to crash down in ruins'. This was an apt metaphor while they were building the tower and spire. By 1325 Bishop Roger was in despair. He pointed out that 28 of the 52 members of his chapter had been provided by popes: the dean, one archdeacon and six prebendaries had been appointed by Pope Clement V; and the treasurer, precentor, an archdeacon and seventeen prebendaries, by Pope John XXII. Furthermore, eight more 'expectant canons' were awaiting prebends! Most of these 'canons' were also Italian and French cardinals who never came anywhere near Salisbury! English royal clerks and university students also petitioned the pope for provision to Salisbury prebends. Many were successful, and they were mostly non-resident too. Despite this, Bishop Roger produced a set of statutes for the cathedral, which reviewed the whole field of cathedral legislation.

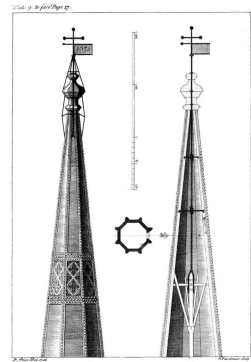

Elevation and Section of the upper part of the Spire with it's Plan just below the weather Door.

Francis Price's drawing of the top of the spire, showing the original ironwork that tied the top of the timber-frame to the capstones and external cross.

A section through the masonry at the top of the spire, drawn full size on the wall of the north aisle of the nave, perhaps by the original designer for a template.

OPPOSITE: Bishop Roger Martival's tomb on the north side of the presbytery, with miniature flying buttresses on it.

Bishop Roger died on 14 March 1330, and a very fine tomb was made for him on the north side of the presbytery, opposite his predecessor's tomb. It shows visually what Bishop Roger had achieved for the cathedral, both metaphorically and literally. The exquisite, thin canopy is covered in Decorated-style tracery with a wonderful series of figures reclining on the main ogee arch. On either side are a whole series of miniature gables, buttresses, finials and flying buttresses, and surmounting the whole is a very elaborate flying-buttressed structure, which has almost been compressed into two dimensions, and looks a bit like a medieval drawing (see p.97). Here is a very fitting way to commemorate a man who had completed the tower and spire and, for stability, had provided it with a whole series of flying buttresses. It also shows a bishop who had come to terms with the difficult political situation in the early fourteenth century, and had given his resident chapter important revised statutes to 'buttress' and support the chapter in the future.

After the death of Bishop Roger, Robert Wyville was appointed in his place. From now on, bishops of Salisbury would be 'civil servants' provided by the pope in collaboration with the royal government in England. Bishop Robert was an able young man who, amazingly, was to remain bishop for more than 45 years (1330–75), although this was entirely within the even longer reign of King Edward III (1327–77). The new bishop, although previously a canon of Lichfield and Lincoln, was a very different man from his predecessors, and this is perhaps best shown by his remarkable gravestone, which now lies in the north-east transept (the so-called 'Morning Chapel'). It was put here in 1684 when the presbytery floor was repaved in black and white marble. Originally it lay in the floor just above the presbytery step, between the

two beautiful tombs of his two predecessors described above (see drawing at top of p.61). Unlike his two predecessors, who had small early brasses on their tomb-chests, Bishop Robert chose to have a vast single slab of Purbeck marble put in the floor, into which was laid one of the largest monumental brasses in England. In the centre the bishop is shown looking out

Fourteenth-century High Street (north) Gate, showing the 15th-century crenellated top.

Robert Wyville's brass

This brass rubbing by Edward Kite was published in 1860. Around the edge of this brass is a long inscription that tells us that he had:

… gathered together the dispersed possessions of the church [of Salisbury] and, having so collected, as a vigilant pastor he prudently maintained the same, for among the least of his benefits, he recovered like an intrepid champion the Castle of Sherborne to the said church, which for 200 years and more had been withheld therefrom by military violence. He also procured the restoration to the same church of its Chase of Bere.

from a large castle while, beneath him and standing outside the portcullised main gate, is his champion Richard Shawell. To the right and left of Shawell's feet, rabbits can be seen scuttling into their burrows.

The brass depicts the most famous event in the bishop's life when, at Westminster in 1355, he successfully recovered Sherborne Castle (lost to the see in 1139) and the Chase at Bere in Berkshire (hence the rabbit warren on the brass). The fact that the bishop came very close to a trial by battle to recover them shows how the scholarly world of the early fourteenth-century bishops had now evolved into the chivalric world of King Edward III. With the outbreak of the Hundred Years War in 1337, Bishop Robert was 'licensed to crenellate' his palace at Salisbury and his London house in Fleet Street, as well as several other key manorial residences at places like Woodford, Chardstock, Potterne, Bishop's Canning and Sonning.

Interestingly enough, a licence to crenellate the Close of Salisbury was given ten years earlier, in August 1327, but this was because of the poor relations between the canons and the town. The Close wall had been built along the north and north-east sides in the thirteenth century, but it was only after 1327 that the wall top was crenellated and the High Street Gate and St Ann's Gate were fully fortified. (In the fifteenth century, relations with the town became so bad that a portcullis was added to the outside of the High Street Gate.) After 1337 the bishop fortified his own gatehouse on Exeter Street and crenellated his portion of the Close wall to the south. The canons then continued the building of the Close wall beyond this, and we know that in 1342 the chapter agreed that the high churchyard wall should be reduced to provide stone for the new work on the Close wall. While all this was going on, the bishop also allowed a large bank and ditch to be built on the vulnerable north and east sides of the town (but, despite a new licence to crenellate in 1372, no stone wall). Because of the low-lying meadow-land and the river Avon on the west and south, no defences were built here, and even the southern Close wall was not fully completed.

Luckily the magnificent spire had just been completed before the dean and chapter, and the citizens of Salisbury, had turned their attention to expensive fortification works, and before the bishop became caught up in Edward III's royal court and French wars. Even worse was the dreadful plague, known as the Black Death, which reached the Dorset coast in August 1348 and spread rapidly across the diocese, killing up to half the population. This was only a temporary setback to the very successful town of New Salisbury, but it left many of the rural areas around the city depopulated.

Flying buttresses in the nave clerestory and triforium – some of many that support the upper crossing piers on the north-west.

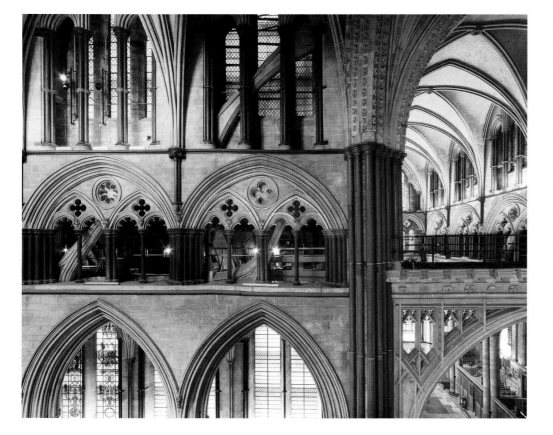

9

THE LATE MIDDLE AGES, TUDOR AND EARLY STUART PERIODS

With the completion of the tower, spire and, to a lesser extent, the defences of the Close, the building work at Salisbury Cathedral was seen as complete. However, quite a lot of new building work was undertaken in the later fifteenth century, which should still be considered. Unfortunately, though, most of this work at the east end, around the new shrine of St Osmund, was destroyed in 1789–90 during James Wyatt's restoration.

On 23 April 1445, in Titchfield Abbey near Southampton, the 23-year-old king, Henry VI, married Margaret of Anjou (who was only sixteen), and the officiating bishop was the king's confessor, William Aiscough, who had been the bishop of Salisbury since 1438. Not long before the wedding, a document tells us that the king had encouraged the building of a new library at Salisbury, which was 'for the keeping of the books to the said Church belonging and also for the increase of science and of virtue of such as will look and study in the same'. This was an early use of the word 'science', meaning knowledge.

LEFT: View of the remaining part of the library from the cloister garth.

RIGHT: The masonry bridge leading to the library in the south-west corner of the south transept.

At the same time, the cathedral's Chapter Act Book records that it was thought desirable:

> … for divers reasons to have suitable schools for lectures, together with a library for the safe-keeping of books, and the convenience of those who wish to study them, which library shall be built as soon as possible over one side of the cloister of the church, at the cost of William now bishop of Salisbury, the dean and the canons of the aforesaid church.

It was at this time that Oxford University was starting to build the fine new library over the Divinity School, to house a new collection of books donated by Duke

Humphrey of Gloucester. This building in Oxford is now literally at the core of the Bodleian Library. This is no coincidence because the canon treasurer of Salisbury at this time was Gilbert Kymer, who was also the chancellor of Oxford University and physician to Henry VI and Duke Humphrey. In 1449 Gilbert became dean of Salisbury, and the work on the new library, over the east cloister walk, must now have been nearing completion. It is recorded that the work was to be super-vised by four scholar-canons: Gilbert himself and Nicholas Upton (the precentor), William Ingram and Thomas Cyrceter. The last of these canons left many sermons and manuscripts to the library in his will.

This fine building, which occupied the whole of the very long space above the east cloister walk, was entered by a little masonry bridge from the spiral staircase in the south-west corner of the south transept. Just above the inside of the main doorway into the library are beautifully carved corbel heads of a king and a bishop. These are presumably of Henry VI (now partly obscured by a bookcase) and William Aiscough. Alas, Bishop Aiscough was brutally murdered by a mob on 29 June 1450 during the Jack Cade rebellion, when he was at Edington, and all his manors were looted. The Salisbury library, his memorial, is still here, but in 1758 the chapter ordered the southern part of the library to be taken down and the books to be relocated in the northern section.

Very soon after Bishop Aiscough's murder, the recently appointed bishop of Hereford, Richard Beauchamp, was rapidly translated to Salisbury. This new young bishop, a local Wiltshire man, had known Henry VI since they were both children. He had also been involved with the building of the Divinity School and library at Oxford, where he was a doctor of canon

Engraving by R. Thacker, c.1675, of the cathedral from the south-west. On the right, the whole of the lecture theatre and library (above the east cloister) is shown, while the bell-tower with its timber-and-lead covered spire is visible on the left.

law. Beauchamp's 30 years as bishop of Salisbury were highly effective ones, even though they coincided with the bitter 'Wars of the Roses' (1453–71).

Since the late fourteenth century, much time and money had been spent on trying, once again, to bring about the canonisation of Bishop Osmund, but it was only after 1452, when Bishop Beauchamp vigorously took up the cause with the Pope in Rome, that success was finally achieved, and on 1 January 1457 the very elderly and austere Spanish Pope, Callistus III, formally canonised St Osmund. Much of the documentation for this survives in the cathedral archives, and Callistus's 'Bull of Canonisation' orders that the tomb of St Osmund should be 'set up in a more worthy place in order that the multitude of the faithful in Christ may visit it freely'.

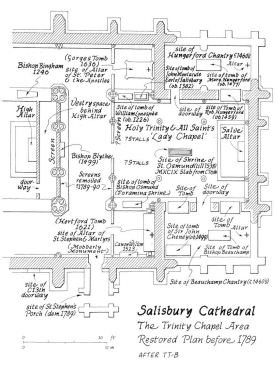

Salisbury Cathedral
The Trinity Chapel Area
Restored Plan before 1789
AFTER TT-B

Reconstructed plan of the east end during the late Middle Ages, showing the chantry chapels and tombs removed in 1789.

Perhaps already begun in 1456, a magnificent shrine was quickly built in the centre of the Trinity Chapel. Then, on 16 July 1457, a great feast of 'translation' took place, during which the remains (now sacred relics) of St Osmund were taken out of the tomb on the south side and placed in a new 'Cofyn of Tymbre' in the 'feretory' on top of the magnificent shrine. Much decoration, including gold and jewels, was added to the shrine over the next few decades, and many pilgrims came to visit it, no doubt encouraged by the indulgences granted them by the Pope. Two of the cathedral canons were made 'the keepers of the offerings and jewels and things pertaining to the shrine of St Osmund'. Henry VI is known to have brought a 'golden tablet' (*unam tabulam auream*), on which was the image of the Trinity studded with 43 great pearls and eleven blue precious stones. It remained in place for a mere 80 years, until Henry VIII ordered its destruction (along with all other shrines in England) in 1538. Today the site is marked by a black Tournai marble slab upon which is the date MXCIX (1099).

As we have seen already, the Trinity Chapel acted as the Lady Chapel of the cathedral, in which the daily Lady Mass was celebrated. By the later fifteenth century, very elaborate polyphonic Lady Masses were sung there by a professional choir of boys and men (the forerunner to the present cathedral choir), and special stalls would have been built for them near the shrine. Unfortunately, all traces of these stalls were also removed after the Reformation, but Winchester Cathedral still contains Lady Chapel choir stalls of this date.

Trinity Chapel, detail of the reused fan-vaults from the Beauchamp chantry chapel (see following page), which were installed there in 1789.

OPPOSITE AND ABOVE: The fine carved head-stops of a bishop and a king just inside the library door.

Bishop Beauchamp's chantry chapel looking east, just before its demolition. Sir John Cheney's tomb (and effigy) is on the right.

Hungerford chantry chapel looking east, just before its demolition in 1789. It is possible to see that the tombs are already being removed.

Various other changes and additions were made to the east end of the cathedral after the new shrine was added here. Luckily we still have an early eighteenth-century plan of the cathedral (see p.119) and some other early views, which give us an impression of some of this work. Most striking of all are the two external chantry chapels added on either side of the Trinity Chapel, for the Hungerfords (on the north) and for Bishop Beauchamp. Beauchamp's chapel, in which he was buried in 1481, was an exceptionally splendid miniature structure in the late Gothic style, which faced south to the new chamber block at the bishop's palace. Immediately to the west of the chapel, a new doorway and porch (known as St Stephen's Porch) was made into the east end of the south choir aisle. It was no doubt used by the bishop himself and the more important visitors to the shrine.

South side of Bishop Audley's chantry chapel, c.1520. The tomb-chest on the right was also used as the Easter Sepulchre, as it lay immediately north of the high altar.

In addition to the external (now demolished) chantry chapels, one early Tudor bishop, Edmund Audley (1502–24), built a superb miniature internal chantry chapel just to the north of the high altar. This fine structure has fortunately survived; it is covered by a fan-vault (see p.4) and still retains some of its original decoration.

Before the reordering of 1789–90, the high altar must have been raised to a considerable height, with a large stone screen behind it. Immediately above the high altar itself was an exquisite statue of the Blessed Virgin Mary, which was the focal point of the whole cathedral, but particularly for the services in the choir and presbytery. Behind the high altar screen, which may have been at least twenty feet (6 m) high during the late medieval period (like the surviving screen in Winchester Cathedral), was a long, narrow vestry with another screen on its east side. Built into

the east side of this screen was the tomb-chest of Bishop John Blythe (1494–9), surmounted by the bishop's effigy. This structure was relocated to the north wall of the north transept in 1790, when the whole area between the choir stalls and the Trinity Chapel was opened up as one very long 'worship space' – a great mistake, as was quickly discovered. What a contrast to the final phase before the Reformation, when the main daily worship took place in the choir and presbytery, while hidden behind the great screen was the inner 'jewelbox' of the Trinity Chapel, with its shrine of St Osmund and the glorious sounds and smells of the daily polyphonic Lady Mass!

After Bishop Beauchamp had achieved the canonisation of St Osmund in 1457, he was sent on several diplomatic missions for Henry VI and Queen Margaret in 1458–9. Soon after this he was caught up in the civil wars that plagued the next decade. After the final battles in 1471, he emerged as a key supporter of King Edward IV, and from 1475 until his death in 1481, he was given the job of building the remarkable new private royal chapel of St George in Windsor Castle; this was to be Edward IV's own burial place and chantry chapel. Beauchamp was also made dean of Windsor and was appointed to the new office of chancellor of the Order of the Garter. He was clearly a busy man and not often in Salisbury. However, it is in these last years of the bishop's life (1479–81) that we have the building of the splendid lierne vault over the crossing in Salisbury Cathedral. Before this, there was only a wooden ceiling there, which had been erected in the late fourteenth century. It is also fortunate that the earliest surviving detailed fabric accounts for the cathedral date from this time, and they also tell us about the costs

The lierne vault that was put over the crossing in the last year of Bishop Beauchamp's life. On it are the arms of various people who may have helped pay for it in 1479–81.

of preparatory work; the putting in of the 'syntryn' (centring) to support the ribs of the new vault; and the bringing in of new Hazelbury stone (from near Box in North Wiltshire) for making the ribs themselves. There is also mention of stone for a new *archebuttan* (or flying buttress) to the tower, and luckily we can still see this rebuilt flying buttress, made of Hazelbury stone, outside the north-east corner of the tower. This is one final, but very obscure, monument to Bishop Beauchamp's last year as bishop of Salisbury.

By the 1520s Salisbury Cathedral was in its final 'golden age' before the Reformation. But when Bishop Audley died in 1524 and was buried beneath his elegant chantry chapel beside the high altar, his successor was the Italian Cardinal, Lorenzo Campeggio, who had been provided by the pope, with the agreement of Henry VIII. This great renaissance cardinal came to England to assist Cardinal Wolsey with the king's 'great matter', the royal divorce. After the break with Rome, Campeggio was deprived of the see, in 1535, by an

Act of Parliament. In Rome, however, he continued to be regarded as bishop of Salisbury until his death, and even then an 'anti-bishop of Salisbury' was appointed there.

Campeggio's replacement was Nicholas Shaxton, a Cambridge evangelical who was Anne Boleyn's almoner; she was now Henry VIII's new queen. Shaxton introduced Bible reading in English and preaching to the cathedral. He was also Salisbury's first married bishop and an old friend of Archbishop Thomas Cranmer (who was also 'secretly' married), but in July 1539 he was forced to resign his see. The next bishop, John Capon, was another Cambridge theologian and Benedictine monk, whose brother had been Cardinal Wolsey's chaplain. In 1539 he was bishop of Bangor and abbot of Hyde Abbey in Winchester. He surrendered the abbey to Henry VIII on 30 April, and three months later he was made bishop of Salisbury. Capon was notorious for his 'changes in religion' and survived both the great Protestant changes under King Edward VI (1547–53) and the reversion to Catholicism under 'Bloody' Queen Mary. He died just before Mary, on 6 October 1557, and his *ex situ* tomb-chest can be seen on the bench on the south-east side of the choir. Although Bishop Capon had a bad reputation as a time-server, it should be noted that in 1542, under Archbishop Cranmer, the Sarum Use became compulsory throughout the province of Canterbury. Recent dendrochronology has shown that the eastern part of the nave roof and the whole of the south transept roof were completely rebuilt with fine new oak timbers in the same year. The thirteenth-century roofs had racked badly, so the new roofs are notable for their use of double tiers of wind-braces to stop any future racking.

During the early 1540s, the frequently absentee dean was an Italian, Peter Vannes.

Part of the roof over the nave, dating to 1542, which shows the wind braces against the rafters to prevent racking. The tie-beams in the foreground were replaced with bolted 4-ply timbers in the 1930s because no new 35-feet-long oak tie-beams could be purchased!

As he was often busy in his other role as the king's Latin secretary, he was often represented in Salisbury by the precentor, Dr Thomas Bennett, another well-known time-server like the bishop. He had a magnificent monument built for himself on the north-east side of the choir in 1554, four years before his death.

When Queen Elizabeth succeeded to the throne in 1558, morale in the Close was at a low ebb and its new bishop, the 38-year-old John Jewel (1560–71), found 'very many things amiss, which we took grievously to heart'. Many of the Close houses were in a poor state, and the spire was said to be in need of repair after a major lightning strike, which the bishop claimed had made a fissure 'from the top for 60 feet downwards'. When he wrote this, in a letter to his friend Peter Martyr in Zurich, he had not yet seen the cathedral (he was enthroned, by proxy, on 6 March 1560), and it is very likely that the '60-foot fissure' (18 m) was, in fact, in the lead on the spire over the bell-tower, not in the cathedral's magnificent stone spire. The interior of the cathedral was also in a poor state; it was described as being 'in great ruin', needing £2,000 worth of repairs. The stone altars had been taken down for a second time in 1559 (the first had been in 1550), and they were replaced with plain wooden tables once more. There was also a second sale of jewels, ornaments and copes, and also much destruction of the imagery of the saints in the stained-glass windows. The Fabric Accounts tell us of payments for boarding up and reglazing various windows. However, Bishop Jewel and his successor Edmund Gheast (1571–7) did much to repair the building and to put it in good order. We know, for example, that Bishop Jewel's name and arms were found in many of the windows in the nave, which was now being furnished with 'high' fixed seating around a pulpit. The Mayor and Corporation attended services on Sunday, although there were increasing squabbles between the City and the wives and families of the clergy, over the placing of pews and consequently questions of precedence. This was finally dealt with in 1634, when Archbishop Laud ordered the pews' removal, with only movable seats being allowed. Queen Elizabeth I disapproved of married clergy living in the Close, but was unable to stop this practice. Moreover, by the early seventeenth century, Salisbury had become a fashionable centre and King James I came to stay in the Close on eight separate occasions, either at the 'King's House' (formerly the abbot of Sherborne's house) or in the Bishop's Palace. As a result, the cathedral and Close were thoroughly cleaned and flowers and perfumes were purchased for 'dressing His Majesty's seat' in the choir. A substantial sum was also spent on ensuring the services' music was of a high standard.

Dr Thomas Bennett's cadavered effigy on his tomb-chest in a recess in the screen on the north-east side of the choir. He had been Cardinal Wolsey's chaplain and the vicar-general of the diocese (for the absent Cardinal Campeggio), before becoming precentor in 1536. Note Bennett's initials and 'DL' (Doctor of Law) on the tomb-chest.

Although the fabric and furnishings of the cathedral was now much improved, there was a great deal of unrest in the City and Close, which continued until the start of the Civil War in 1642. Despite this, the services and music were mostly of a high standard and loved by the famous poet George Herbert, who came over from his rectory at nearby Bemerton, between 1630 and his death in 1633. The largely Puritan citizens of Salisbury, who were now in the ascendant, condemned it for being 'too formal and curious'. Despite this, the Great organ, which had been positioned on the pulpitum screen over the entrance to the choir in 1539, was substantially enlarged in 1635 and was given an extra Choir organ. At the same time, some large secular monuments were erected in the cathedral to cover the tombs of some of the greatest local landowners. These monuments, such as the one to the Gorges (of Longford Castle) at the east end of the north presbytery aisle – and the Hertford monument in a similar position on the south – were deliberately placed on the sites of medieval altars.

In 1612 an important change took place in Salisbury, when the king freed the City from the overlordship of the bishop, and granted it a Charter of Incorporation. He also gave the Close and its 'liberty' their own Charter, providing them with separate jurisdiction and the right to have their own pillory, tumbrel, stocks and prison (situated near the High Street Gate).

During the Civil War, there was much violent unrest in the city in 1644 and 1645, and on one occasion a minor siege took place around the bell-tower, when Royalists set fire to the south door of the tower, to smoke out the parliamentary troops inside. Fortunately the fabric of the cathedral was not too badly damaged during this time, although, most likely, a lot of lead was removed from the roof.

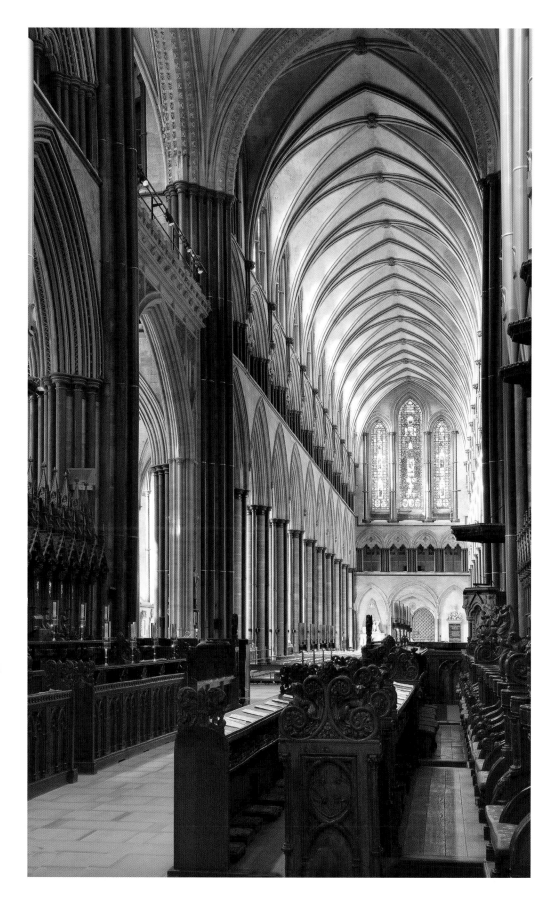

OPPOSITE: View west from the choir stalls into the nave. Until the 19th century, this view was blocked by a stone screen with the organ on it.

A reconstructed plan of the Cathedral Close in the early 16th century.

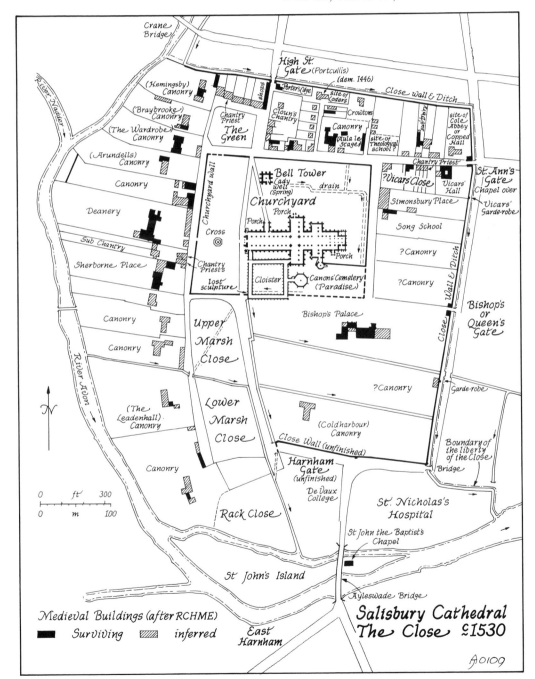

Crane Bridge

River Nadder

High St. Gate (Portcullis) (dem. 1446)

shops

(Hemingsby) Canonry

(Braybrooke) Canonry

Chantry Priest

(The Wardrobe) Canonry

The Green

(Arundells) Canonry

Canonry

Deanery

Sub Chantry

Sherborne Place

Churchyard Wall

Chantry Priests

lost sculpture

Cross

Canonry

Canonry

Upper Marsh Close

River Avon

(The Leadenhall) Canonry

Lower Marsh Close

Canonry

Close Wall (unfinished)

Harnham Gate (unfinished)

De Vaux College

Rack Close

Close Wall & Ditch

Porters lodge

site of Loders

Cloun's Chantry

Crowtons

Canonry

Aula le Stage

site of Theological school?

Bell Tower (Lady well (spring)

drain

Churchyard

Porch

Porch

Cloister

Porch

Canons' Cemetery (Paradise)

Bishop's Palace

?Canonry

(Coldharbour) Canonry

?Canonry

Vicars' Close

Vicars' Hall

Simonsbury Place

Song School

?Canonry

?Canonry

St. Ann's Gate

Chapel over

Vicars' Garde-robe

Close Wall & Ditch

Bishop's or Queen's Gate

Garde-robe

Boundary of the liberty of the Close

Bridge

Chantry Priest

site of Cole Abbey or Copped Hall

Sudbury

St. Nicholas's Hospital

St John the Baptist's Chapel

St John's Island

East Harnham

Ayleswade Bridge

Medieval Buildings (after RCHME)

■ Surviving   ▨ inferred

0   ft   300
0   m   100

N

Salisbury Cathedral
The Close c.1530

A0109

In 1648 an Act of Parliament abolished the dean and chapter. The following year, another Act provided for the sale of the lands belonging to deans and chapters. Most of the canons, as Royalists, had left the Close several years before, but a most interesting survey (dated 5 August 1649) gives us a detailed description of the Close at this time. Each canon's 'mansion house' is fully described, as are all the other houses, including the six 'dwelling houses of the late Vicar's Chorall' and the seven houses of lay vicars. The mayor of Salisbury was now in charge of the Close, and the City Corporation decided to buy four of the canons' houses for £800, as permanent residences for the four Presbyterian ministers of the City. One of these was the minister at the cathedral, and it was ordered that he 'preacheth twice in the Cathedral every Lord's Day', and that 'Our Ladye churche be made a parish churche'. Therefore, services were not quite at an end, but this was probably the lowest point in the cathedral's long history.

We also know that, for a time, the cloisters were converted into a prison, with Dutch prisoners being kept there in 1653. The mayor wrote to the government begging for their removal, saying that some had escaped and that much damage had already been caused to the cloister piers and to the library windows above. During this time, it is almost certain that virtually all the glazing was ripped out from the upper sections of the cloister arcades, making the cloister walks much more vulnerable to driving rain. Amazingly, the glazing has never been put back. Despite this, and compared to many other English cathedrals at this time, the cathedral fabric seems to have been fairly well maintained by the richer members of the gentry in Salisbury.

However, one building that was very badly damaged was the magnificent medieval Bishop's Palace. This had been completely rebuilt by Bishop Beauchamp in the 1450s, and now, after two centuries, the whole structure was pulled down, apart from Bishop Beauchamp's porch and chamber block, with the thirteenth-century undercroft behind it. The Parliamentarians had a particular hatred of the bishops, and this destruction of their palaces was almost universal in England. After the Restoration, as we shall see in the next chapter, the bishops had to start anew. Luckily, the bishops of Salisbury were then able to reacquire their large incomes, and by the early nineteenth century, the palace was once again a magnificent mansion set in a beautiful contrived landscape created for Bishop John Fisher, which was superbly depicted by John Constable in *Salisbury Cathedral from the Bishop's Grounds.* (opposite).

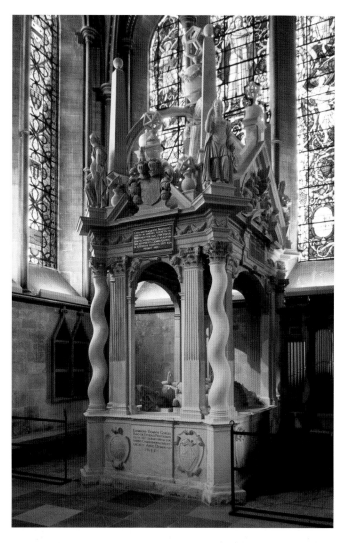

Gorges monument at the east end of the north choir aisle.

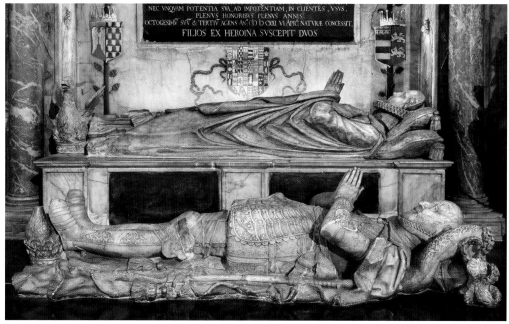

The main effigies on the Hertford monument.

John Constable's magnificent view of the cathedral 'from the bishop's grounds', painted in 1823. In the left foreground is Bishop John Fisher and his wife and daughter.

10

RESTORATION

In 1660 Charles II returned to England, arriving at Dover on 25 May. Soon after this date, the bishops, deans and chapters of all the English cathedrals were restored. Bishop Duppa was translated from Salisbury to Winchester, and the precentor, Humphrey Henchman, was appointed bishop. The other surviving members of the old chapter quickly set in hand the restoration of the institutions and worship in the cathedral, and a new 'Holy Table', with rails around it, was immediately installed on the site of the old high altar. Many new canons (or prebendaries as they were now called) had to be appointed quickly, but the dean, Dr Richard Bailey (1635–67), was the one figure of continuity. The dean and chapter concentrated initially on refurbishing the building. The fine Thomas Harris organ was reinstated on top of the choir screen in 1661. (It had been removed in 1643, just before the Puritans descended on the cathedral to smash it up.) Also a striking new classical font was bought in London in 1662, for £2 12s and set up at the west end of

the nave. Other lesser items such as plate and song books were also purchased at this time, and Bishop Duppa donated a generous sum of £500 towards the cost of the new work.

Bishop Duppa's vicar-general, Thomas Hyde, was also a prebendary of Salisbury and, with his family, had discreetly looked after the fabric of the cathedral in the 1650s. This was partly an act of piety because the family, who lived at Heale House near Salisbury, had quietly buried Sir Henry Hyde in the cathedral after his execution in 1650. The monument in the south nave aisle, erected soon after 1660, refers to him as finishing life 'kissing the axe…to suffer the envied martyrdom of Charles I'. Two other brothers were buried in the cathedral, one who was briefly bishop in 1665–7.

After the death of Bishop Hyde, another very distinguished but very different man, Dr Seth Ward, was made bishop of Salisbury, having been bishop of Exeter. Most famously, he brought in his friend Dr Christopher Wren to do a survey, in

The rebuilt central pier, repainted vaults and reglazing of the chapter house, 1856–60.

August 1668, of the ruined palace and of the cathedral's fabric. Most of Wren's suggestions were carried out in the next 50 years or so, and in 1719 (not long before Wren's death) most of his survey was published in the first ever book on the cathedral: *History and Antiquities of Salisbury*, by Richard Rawlinson.

The choir was completely refurbished in 1671–2 with Wren acting as adviser and designer. The original medieval stalls were kept, but fine new carved and painted wooden screens were put around the backs of the stalls, and many embellishments were added to make a handsome baroque space. Sadly, all of this was stripped out in 1777, but a little of the panelling can still be seen in a house in the Close, and the elaborate front of Dean Brideoak's stall is now in the north-east transept. He worked closely and well with Bishop Ward, but when he became bishop of Chichester, a difficult new dean, Thomas Pierce (1675–91), was appointed, who was to cause Ward many problems and eventually to drive him to a breakdown. In 1676–7 parts of the nave were repaved and inward-facing new pews were put into the eastern half. This would allow the whole congregation to enter the nave to hear the sermon, and a pulpit was probably erected nearby. In 1684 Dr Robert Townton, a prebendary and son of a former bishop, paid for the choir and presbytery to be completely repaved in black-and-white marble. Before this took place, the most prominent grave slabs (including Bishop Wyville's great brass-covered slab of 1375)

Bishop Seth Ward

Seth Ward had been Savilian Professor of Astronomy at Oxford and a founder member of the Royal Society. His 22 years in Salisbury saw him taking a very active part in the refurnishing and beautifying of the cathedral for services. He donated large sums towards a whole series of projects, such as the repaving of the great cloister's east walk; the remodelling of the choir stalls; and the making of a new bishop's throne in 1672. He also started to rebuild the ruined bishop's palace in order to transform it once again into a fine residence, and he helped rebuild the guildhall in the town. Sir Christopher Wren (who succeeded Ward as Savilian Professor) wrote a masterly report on the cathedral for the bishop in 1668, which describes the 'large and magnificent pile' that, he said, 'may be justly accounted one of the best patterns of architecture in yt age wherein it was built'. Wren then enumerated its defects and suggested various remedies for its better preservation – all of them very practical.

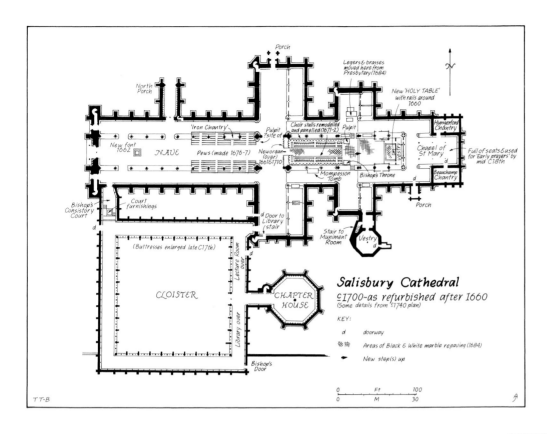

Salisbury Cathedral
c1700~as refurbished after 1660
(Some details from *c1740 plan)

KEY:

d   doorway

※⊞   Areas of Black & White marble repaving (1684)

→   New step(s) up

were moved to the north-east transept. By the time this was done, most of the work of beautifying the cathedral had been completed. By the time of Bishop Ward's death on 6 January 1689, England had changed greatly, following the death of Charles II in 1685, and the 'Glorious Revolution' of 1688. In his will, the bishop donated many books to the cathedral library, and a generous gift of £1,000 for the upkeep of the fabric of the cathedral. His magnificent monument has both a mitred bust of the bishop on it and an exceptional marble carving of his scientific instruments.

By the early eighteenth century the cathedral was once again at a high point, under the distinguished Scottish bishop, Gilbert Burnet (1689–1715). Many of the prebendaries were very able and learned men (scientists as well as theologians), and

OPPOSITE AND BELOW: Bishop Seth Ward's scientific instruments, carved in marble, and his mitred bust set on his monument in the south-east transept.

The top of the 1672 dean's stall. The desk is flanked by two carved oak trees, which are clasped by pairs of hands – the punning rebus of Dean Ralph Brideoak (1667–75). This was carved by Alexander Fort, who was a master joiner from Salisbury and one of Wren's craftsmen.

the vestry even contained a barometer. The Close was now full of fine new (or rebuilt) houses and a distinguished new school-house, which was built for the choristers in 1716–17. A few years before this, a magnificent new organ was built on top of the choir screen by Renatus Harris (see engraving on p.116). This superb instrument, which was the first in England to have four manuals (keyboards), was completed in 1710.

In 1734 the bishop of Bangor and a former vice-chancellor of Cambridge, Thomas Sherlock, was translated to Salisbury and when, after a year in the palace, he decided that it needed enlarging and beautifying, he brought in a man called Francis Price to design and build some new rooms for him. In 1733 Price had published a book called *The British Carpenter, or a Treatise on Carpentry*, which was recommended by several prominent architects (Nicholas Hawksmoor, John James and James Gibbs) as 'a very Usefull and Instructive Piece'. At the Bishop's Palace, his masterpiece was a design for a very fine roof over a new 'Great Dining Room' (on the first floor above the thirteenth-century vaulted under-croft), which had a magnificent plastered coved ceiling suspended from it. This was made in 1736, and soon afterwards Bishop Sherlock recommended Price to the dean and chapter as their surveyor and clerk of works. He made a general survey of all the roofs in the cathedral, some of which were in poor condition. Over the next few years he carried out many repairs and put in completely new roofs over the high eastern arm and along most of the south triforium. He also used Wren's survey as the basis for a more detailed study of the fabric of the whole cathedral, including the spire. In 1753, the year of his death, Price published a pioneering book on the cathedral, and he was probably responsible for the first

measured plan of the cathedral, later entitled 'An Ichnographical Plan of the Cathedral Church of Salisbury'.

Unfortunately, the huge timber-and-lead belfry and spire were not thought worth repairing, as they were 'neither useful nor ornamental', and in 1758 they were ordered to be taken down and all the lead was sold. Four years later, when the work had not been completed, six bells were also sold. Francis Price had made a design in 1746 for a new domed bell-chamber on top of the bell-tower (see p.73), but this was never made. Consequently, the ringing of bells (except mechanically as clock chimes) came to an end and, to this day, Salisbury Cathedral is the only medieval cathedral without bell-ringers. Another demolition ordered in 1758 was of the mid-fifteenth-century library over the southern end of the east-cloister walk. Before this, the roof was rebuilt (at a lower level) on the lecture room over the northern end of the cloister, and the room was fitted out with cases for the books. A few years after this, in 1762, some repairs were made to the spire, and four very small oval windows containing glass were created halfway up the spire. At the same time, a new 'great wheel' (windlass) was made at the base of the spire to replace the worn out original one. It is still in working condition, but was finally replaced by an electric winch towards the end of the twentieth century.

The most drastic changes, however, took place in two main stages in the fifteen years between 1777 and 1792. Firstly, under Bishop John Hume (1766–82), the cathedral was closed for nearly two years

The great wheel at the base of the spire, which was made by Edmund Lush in 1762 to replace the medieval one. Until about 1985, it was used to raise all materials from the crossing floor to a height of about 220 feet (67 m).

Title page of Francis Price's book
With its cumbersome title, this was the first book on a large English Gothic cathedral which described and analysed the fabric. It was illustrated with many of Price's own measured drawings, which are still invaluable today.

A
SERIES
Of particular and useful
OBSERVATIONS,
Made with great Diligence and Care, upon that
ADMIRABLE STRUCTURE,
THE
Cathedral-Church of Salisbury.
CALCULATED
For the Use and Amusement of GENTLEMEN, and other curious PERSONS, as well as for the Assistance of such ARTISTS as may be employed in Buildings of the like Kind : By all which they will be enabled to form a right Judgment upon this, or any ancient Structure, either in the Gothick or other Stiles of Building.

By FRANCIS PRICE,
Author of the BRITISH CARPENTER.

LONDON:
Printed by C. and J. ACKERS, in St. John's-Street;
And Sold by R. BALDWIN, at the Rose in Pater-Noster-Row.
M.DCC.LIII.

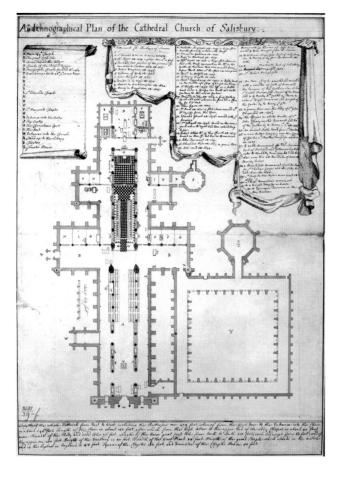

Measured plan of Salisbury Cathedral, perhaps by Francis Price, dating to c.1740.

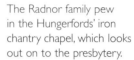

The Radnor family pew in the Hungerfords' iron chantry chapel, which looks out on to the presbytery.

(1777–9) for 'repairing, cleansing and beautifying', under the surveyor Edmund Lush. He had succeeded Francis Price in 1753, and had been in charge of the demolition work already mentioned. Now he was required to remove the nave pulpit and pews, and to make new pews with galleries over them, behind the choir stalls, after the removal of the Wren/Fort panelling. Lush was also ordered to remove the fine thirteenth-century double doorway into the choir from the west, and to extend the presbytery twenty feet into the Trinity Chapel. This was to allow the choir and presbytery to become the only 'worship space' in the cathedral. Lush's job was to make it into a more cosy and intimate theatrical space, within the heart of the cathedral, and it was now made warmer in winter by installing two or three large charcoal braziers. Though the work was not finished until 1779, the cathedral had to be briefly reopened in 1778 for a visit by the king and queen.

Apart from the bishop, one of the more generous sponsors of this work was Jacob Pleydell-Bouverie, second earl of Radnor, who now owned nearby Longford Castle. He decided that he wanted a very grand new family pew, near the bishop, on the south side of this new 'worship space'. To this end, in 1778, he organised for the Hungerfords' fifteenth-century iron chantry chapel to be moved from its original position on the north-east side of the nave to the south side of the presbytery opposite the Audley chantry. Redecorated internally and fitted out with fine individual chairs, it is still occasionally used by the family. Lord Radnor also suggested that a new three-light high east window should be put above the high altar. Unfortunately, the new glass lights were too long, so the original thirteenth-century sills had to be cut out to accommodate the new glass. Remarkably this window is still *in situ* and

Even so must the Son of Man be lifted up.

was not removed by the Victorians, no doubt because of the influence of the later earls of Radnor, who also stopped the removal of their pew in the Victorian restoration (see below).

Bishop Hume died in 1782 and his successor was the bishop of Llandaff, the Hon. Shute Barrington, the youngest son of the Irish first Viscount Barrington. He was also a canon of Windsor and chaplain, and a friend of George III. He was a very wealthy man who liked to live in great state. Soon after the appointment of Bishop Shute Barrington, the Hon. John Byng, while visiting Salisbury, wrote:

The Close is comfortable, and the divines well seated, but the house of God is kept in sad order, to the disgrace of our Church, and of Christianity. The Churchyard is like a cow-common, as dirty and as neglected, and thro' the centre stagnates a boggy ditch. I wonder that the residents do not subscribe to plant near, and rowl the walks, and cleanse the ditch, which might be made a handsome canal. I hope that when the new bishop arrives, who is a scholar, and a gentleman; he will be shock'd at the dilapidation of the beautiful old Chapter house; and the Cloisters; thro' the rubbish of which they are now making a passage for his new Lordship's installation in the Chapter House.

The bishop quickly took the hint, and immediately incorporated the south-eastern part of the churchyard around the chapter house, into his garden. The rest of the huge garden in the south-east corner of the Close was then landscaped, and many new picturesque features were added. In 1783–5, Bishop Barrington brought in the distinguished architect Sir Robert Taylor to redesign his palace entirely, so it could more fittingly entertain the king and royal

family on their next visits. They had last been there briefly in 1778, and from 1789 they called in regularly on their way to the seaside at Weymouth.

Next, the bishop turned to his cathedral and its unsatisfactory setting. In 1786 a new measured plan was made of the churchyard with all its paths, ditches and graves. Soon afterwards the drains were covered over, the ground was levelled, the cemetery was closed and the tombs and tombstones were removed or laid flat under a new grass lawn. Then, in 1789, work began on tidying up the cathedral. Externally, this consisted of removing later excrescences like the eastern chantry chapels and the lesser porches, and most importantly of all, the total removal of the stone bell-tower and all the later buildings around it. For this work, Bishop Barrington brought in and sponsored the most fashionable architect of the day, James Wyatt, who did his first survey on the cathedral in 1787. Wyatt set out many radical proposals for 'improvements', which the dean and chapter finally agreed to on 26 August 1789. The cathedral was closed on 1 October 1789, and remained shut for the next three years, while many articles and letters of protest were published in the *Gentleman's Magazine* and elsewhere, though all to no avail. Fortunately, though, The Society of Antiquaries of London sent the artist Jacob Schnebbelie to make drawings and watercolours during the early part of the work; these are now an invaluable record of many of the demolished features, such as the chantry chapels (see p.104).

The most important 'improvements' were considered to be the tidying up of the cathedral and the removal of clutter, so that one had 'open vistas' throughout to see the 'pure' thirteenth-century Gothic architecture. After the removal of the chantry chapels, the Trinity Chapel (or

OPPOSITE: The new high east window of 1781 depicting Moses and the Brazen Serpent. It was made by James Pearson and was funded by the 2nd Earl of Radnor. It is now a rare survival of 18th-century glass.

J. M. W. Turner, *Salisbury Cathedral Interior, looking towards the North Transept, c.1802–5*, pencil and watercolour. Depicted here is Wyatt's new choir screen (made partly with fragments from the chantry chapels), which is surmounted by George III's new organ.

St Mary's chapel as it was then called) became the new chancel, with everything in the middle (between it and the choir) being stripped out. Almost all the medieval monuments were removed and a selection of the best was roughly reconstructed in neat rows on the arcade benches on either side of the nave, where they still remain. All surviving stained glass was replaced with plain glass, while the walls and vaults were covered with thick layers of limewash. The medieval choir screen was also pulled down, after the Harris organ had been removed from its top, and it was hoped that a new 'open vista' could now be created all the way from the west doors to the Trinity Chapel. Unfortunately for Wyatt and his supporters, including Lord Radnor, the bishop had already persuaded George III to give them a much larger new organ in 1788. Wyatt, therefore, had to build a large new stone screen at the west end of the choir upon which to put it. This blocked the view even more effectively than before, as J. M. W. Turner's wonderful watercolour clearly shows.

Bishop Barrington was translated to Durham in 1791, before the works were completed, and he attempted (less success-fully) to make improvements there. In September 1792, with the work at last finished, the cathedral was reopened to much acclaim. Also, as the *Salisbury Journal* tells us, the king and queen, with the Princess Royal, five other princesses and a small retinue came to the bishop's palace where:

… after partaking of an elegant refection with the bishop and his lady, they visited the Cathedral Church, now quite finished, accompanied by the bishop, the dean and chapter, several prebendaries, the Earl of Pembroke, and Mr Wyatt, who attended to explain the several alterations and improvements, which their Majesties inspected with minute attention, and expressed much satisfaction not only at the elegance and propriety of each, but also at the boldly striking, yet simple and singularly beautiful effect of the *tout ensemble*. The painted window and the new organ excited their particular notice … the Coronation anthem, Hallelujah form the Messiah and other pieces from Handel, to show the different stops, were excellently and judiciously performed by Mr Corfe, the organist, to the great gratification of his Royal auditors.

J. M. W. Turner, *Interior of Salisbury Cathedral, the Choir and Trinity Chapel*, 1797, pencil and watercolour. Visible here is the presbytery after the high altar dais and screens had been removed and replaced by a new altar (with reredos and new glass behind) against the east wall of St Mary's Chapel (the Trinity Chapel).

George III had given the cathedral 1,000 guineas for this magnificent organ, which had been made by Samuel Green of Isleworth, the king's favourite organ builder. The new bishop was John Douglas (1791–1807), who had previously been the dean of Windsor, where a very similar major restoration had just been completed. The canon of Windsor, John Fisher, who was in charge of the restoration there, was to become the next bishop of Salisbury (1807–25) and famously the patron of the artist John Constable.

Nothing very much seems to have happened to the cathedral in the half century or so after 1792, but from the 1830s great reforms were at last starting to take place in the Church of England. Not long before the Cathedrals Act of 1840, a new, very young Bishop Edward Denison, who was appointed in 1837, started the process of revival at Salisbury. He was also the first bishop in the nineteenth century who started to pay for the restoration of fabric, which was once again in poor condition. Worst of all were the chapter house and cloisters, which had not been considered in the eighteenth-century restoration. Small-scale repairs were first carried out in the cloisters in the 1830s. These were organised by a remarkable man called William Osmond, who was both a lay-vicar and a mason. In the 1820s he had started to make some notable Gothic-revival monuments for the cathedral, including the fine monuments for Bishop Fisher and his successor Bishop Thomas Burgess (1825–37), and in 1829–46 Osmond slowly progressed through the cloisters, repairing the roofs (the lead had been replaced with Welsh slates in about 1790) and replacing missing tracery and Purbeck marble shafts with new Chilmark stone shafts.

After Bishop Denison's early death in 1854, it was decided that the chapter house would be completely restored as a memorial to him, and this was overseen by the cathedral architect, Henry Clutton, who was assisted by William Burges. Because Clutton became a Roman Catholic in 1856, he had to resign, and the work was completed under the young George Gilbert Scott. The restoration of the chapter house was initially structural, with the central Purbeck marble pier being completely rebuilt, and the external buttresses underpinned, rebuilt and thickened up. Then all the sculpture inside (particularly the famous frieze) was carefully restored, and the vaults and walls repainted. The tiled floor, which was loose and broken, was wholly replaced with a replica in new Minton tiles. In 1860 new glazing was installed, which roughly followed the medieval style (but without the heraldry). When this started to be removed in 1967, a public outcry managed to stop this process. Long before this, the painting on the walls started to fall off, and the rest was removed before the end of the nineteenth century. Today we feel that the chapter house was over-restored, but in the mid- to later nineteenth century it was highly praised on the whole.

By 1862 Scott had produced a major report on the fabric. This led immediately to a large programme of restoration, which continued until his death in 1878. The work was funded initially with a grant of £10,000 from the Ecclesiastical Commissioners, who had now taken over the cathedral's many estates. Much more money was soon needed, and a public subscription was now put in place, under Bishop Walter Kerr Hamilton (1854–69), who had been one of the most active of the cathedral's reformers. He was brought to Salisbury, from Oxford, by Bishop Denison, and became treasurer, then precentor, before succeeding him as bishop. In 1849 the nave had been opened free to the public from 10.15am to 4pm. After the completion of the chapter house and cloisters, in 1865 these were also made public, together with the choir, for a fee of sixpence, which was payable to the Fabric Fund.

The restoration commenced in 1862–3 on the external stonework, with the tower and spire an early priority; from 1866–9 it concentrated on the west front; and then

work started inside at the east end. The Trinity Chapel was restored and repainted, followed by the rest of the eastern arm, with the high vaults being repainted by 1872, the year Scott was given a knighthood. A completely new high altar dais was created, with an elaborate reredos in 1873. Behind this, an iron screen was erected at the west end of the Trinity Chapel, while south of the high altar Scott designed a fine tomb-chest and effigy for Bishop Kerr Hamilton, after his death in 1869. The choir was also restored from 1869, with the Green organ being removed to St Thomas's Church in the town, and Wyatt's screen being demolished. Many of the medieval fragments from it are now in the lapidarium. Scott wanted to keep the organ on top of a new stone screen, through which one could glimpse the choir from the nave. This was considered too expensive and instead he had to design a magnificent painted iron screen, created by Francis Skidmore of Coventry for £1,000. Sadly this screen was taken out in 1960 and destroyed (except for the gates, which are now in the Victoria and Albert

ABOVE: Reproduction 13th-century monument to Bishop Kerr Hamilton, based on the choir screen of 1236. Designed by G. G. Scott, it was not finished until 1881.

BELOW: Chapter house; the new Purbeck marble central pier base and Minton tile floor of 1856.

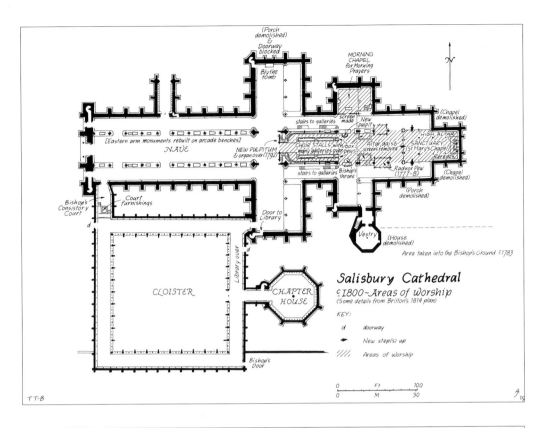

Salisbury Cathedral
c1800~Areas of Worship
(Some details from Britton's 1814 plan)

KEY:
d — doorway
→ — New step(s) up
/// — Areas of Worship

(Porch demolished) & Doorway blocked
Blythe tomb
MORNING CHAPEL for Morning Prayers
stairs to galleries
screen made
New pulpit
(Chapel demolished)
[Eastern arm monuments rebuilt on arcade benches]
NAVE
NEW PULPITUM & organ over (1792)
CHOIR STALLS with box many galleries over pews
Altar dais & screen removed
HIGH ALTAR
SANCTUARY (St Mary's Chapel)
Reredos
stairs to galleries
Bishop's throne
Radnor Pew (1777-8)
(Chapel demolished)
Bishop's Consistory Court
Court furnishings
Door to Library
(Porch demolished)
Vestry
(House demolished)
Area taken into the Bishop's Ground £1783
CLOISTER
CHAPTER HOUSE
Bishop's Door
0 — Ft — 100
0 — M — 30
T T-B

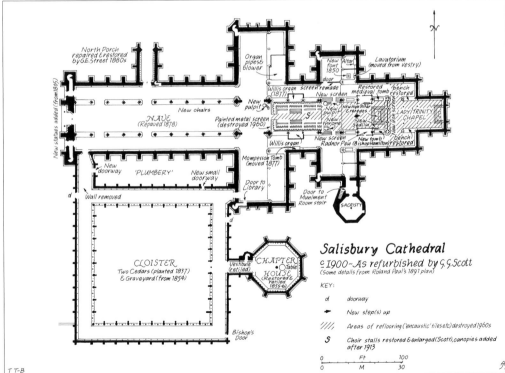

Salisbury Cathedral
c1900~As refurbished by G.G.Scott
(Some details from Roland Paul's 1891 plan)

KEY:
d — doorway
→ — New step(s) up
/// — Areas of reflooring ('encaustic' tiles etc) destroyed 1960s
S — Choir stalls restored & enlarged (Scott), canopies added after 1913

North Porch repaired & restored by G.E.Street 1880s
Organ pipes & blower
New font 1850
Altar
Lavatorium (moved from vestry)
New statues added (from 1865)
NAVE (Repaved 1878)
New chairs
Willis organ screen remade (1877)
New screen
New pulpit
Restored medieval tomb restored
bench restored
Willis organ (1877)
New high altar & reredos
New throne
sedilia
LADY/TRINITY CHAPEL
Painted metal screen (destroyed 1960)
Willis organ
New screen
Radnor Pew (Bishop Hamilton)
New tomb
bench restored
New doorway
'PLUMBERY'
New small doorway
Mompesson Tomb (moved 1877)
Door to Library
Door to Muniment Room stair
Wall removed
SACRISTY
CLOISTER
Two Cedars (planted 1837) & Graveyard (from 1854)
Vestibule (retiled)
Table
CHAPTER HOUSE (Restored & retiled 1855-6)
Bishop's Door
0 — Ft — 100
0 — M — 30
T T-B

Museum). Scott also had the thirteenth-century choir stalls restored, and recreated the medieval north and south doorways into the choir and their associated screens. This work was largely finished by 1875, when work began on the transepts and crossing area. In 1877 the nave was started, and Scott died while the final repaving work was being completed there. A key person in the later part of the work was the dean, Henry Parr Hamilton (1850–80), who appointed George Edmund Street as Scott's successor. He oversaw the restoration of the north porch and the making of the choir-aisle gates, draught-lobbies, gasoliers and other fittings in the 1880s. He was also responsible for the making of the organ cases around the magnificent new Willis organ of 1877. Without a choir screen, the organ was split in two and put on either side of the choir. The organ blower and the 32-foot stop had to be put in the north transept behind Dean Kymer's fine Purbeck marble tomb. After some 25 years of work, over £82,000 had been spent.

In the later nineteenth century, many other 'Victorian' additions were made, of which the most notable were the paving of the choir, presbytery and Trinity Chapel with fine new Minton tiled pavements, and the filling of the eastern arm with a great deal of new stained glass. This process of refurbishment did not come to an end until the 1920s, when canopies were put in place on the back stalls in the choir, and the altars in the transepts were reinstated. Once again small chapels now filled the cathedral, including one (St Margaret's Chapel) 'for women's work and organisations in the diocese'. In the 1930s new altars were even put in front of the Gorges and Hertford monuments at the eastern ends of the choir aisles.

After World War II a reaction against this Victorian need to refurnish every corner soon came, with various fittings and some glass being taken out. This reached a peak in the early 1960s when, under a scheme designed for the dean and chapter by Lord Mottistone, the choir screen and reredos were removed, and all the Victorian tiled pavements were torn out. This was followed by the digging out of many of the graves and archaeological levels beneath them, in the eastern arm, so that an elaborate new under-floor heating system could be put in. Plain machine-cut paving was then put on top of this.

At the end of the twentieth century, after a major public appeal for £6.5 million to 'Save the Spire' had been started in 1987 a very large new repair programme was started, which concentrated first on the tower and spire, and then on the west front. This 'Major Repair Programme' is still in progress and has been greatly assisted by large grants from the government, through English Heritage. Furthermore, there has been a continuing programme of conservation and repair to monuments and to the inside of Salisbury's magnificent great cloister. Some new things are now being installed in the cathedral, including Gabriel Loire's blue 'Prisoners of Conscience' windows in the Trinity Chapel, which were unveiled in 1980 and can now be seen even from the nave; Bishop Barrington's wish for an 'open vista' has, at last, been achieved!

On the eve of Michaelmas Day (Sunday 28 September) 2008, a service was held in the presence of the Archbishop of Canterbury, to celebrate – almost exactly to the day – the 750th anniversary of the consecration of the cathedral on Michaelmas Day, 1258. At the service in 2008, a very large new font in the nave was consecrated and used for the first time by Archbishop Rowan Williams. This is perhaps a fitting start to the new millennium.

LEFT: The southern case in the choir of Father Willis's magnificent new organ of 1876–7.

DO NOT FEAR FOR I HAVE REDEEMED YOU.

LEFT AND OPPOSITE: The new font in the nave, with (left) the trace of a cross made in oil at its consecration by Archbishop Rowan Williams.